A Few Kind Words From a Few Kind People

"This book is SO needed and is SO important. As a busy mother of five who also owns her own business, it's been seriously refreshing to shift my perspective on what's truly important. With a happier and healthy me at the helm, my whole family has benefitted... and my business is thriving!"

CJ Mannix, Certified Hypnotherapist, Pathways To Transformation
Redding, CA

"This is a must-have transformational tool for any woman who has disconnected from herself and her own needs. From a place of authenticity and living real life, Shanti compassionately guides you back to the basics. She created this gift of love that I hope you will take the first step to give to yourself."

Amy AevonAestra Gebo, Corporate Recruiter,
MultiDimensional Healer and Owner Energies to Enlighten
Boston, MA

"There are so many of us women out here struggling, trying to get it all done, and really feeling like we're failing. Shanti has mastered the art of self-care and love without the guilt or shame we usually feel for taking care of ourselves."

JC, University Education Director
Manchester, NH

"I'm taking strides to meet the demands of my life with grace and presence, taking steps to empowering my awesomeness to shine. Thank you, Shanti, for this book and your enlightened guidance."

Stacy Bull, Family Law Paralegal
Concord, NH

EVERYDAY
EASE

EVERYDAY EASE:

Mindfully Moving
From
Burnout To Balance

Shanti Douglas

BE Peace Publishing, LLC

ISBN: 978-1-7326077-0-5

Front cover photo by Bruce Nichols
Front cover photo of Fern Dorresteyn with permission
Graphics from Pixabay.com under CCO free commercial use

Printed in the United States of America

First print edition 2018

BE Peace Publishing, LLC
Concord, NH 03301

www.8limbsHolisticHealth.com

This book is dedicated to all the women mothering the world,
trying their hardest to do their best and make each moment beautiful.
Thank you for giving your Spirit and your energy to those around you,
even when you don't have any left for yourself. I am honored that
you're here now, doing this important work of self-care and self-love,
generating more peace and love in your life.

CONTENTS

1

WHAT'S MY WHY?

All transformational journeys begin with a breakdown.
~ Shanti Douglas ~

In 2007, I resigned from my corporate position as a regional credit manager for one of the world's leading design, engineering and entertainment software development companies. I didn't resign so I could get a life. I resigned to save my life.

You see, I had suspended my sanity to think that what I was doing for work was more important than taking care of myself or my kids (hidden from me in my mind but certainly not hidden in my actions). Progressive adaptation to stress and the desire to succeed professionally in a way that I hadn't succeeded before overshadowed the truth of how lost I really was. The doing of "just one more thing" instigated my familiar phrase of "Hold on!" to any requests at home.

Stress and the perceived importance of my work product crept up on me slowly, slithering into my daily routine so quietly that it went unnoticed. One year, Monday was my favorite workday (all those delicious tasks to master). The next, dread was dragging me out of bed. One year, my walks at lunch were refreshing and part of my self-care routine. The next, they were a midday necessity for unleashing tension and composing my mind so I didn't reactively hit that send button. One year, family meal time was every night. The next, "Did I feed you guys?" One year, it was easy to know what year it was. The next, I questioned the correctness of the calendar (don't laugh - this happened to me all the time).

Don't get me wrong, though. Everything was my choice and it certainly wasn't all bad. I actually loved many parts of what I did and found my job to be engaging, exciting, and empowering. There was always some challenge to address and, with the level of autonomy and responsibility I had, it felt great to think I was making a difference and creating change, even if it was corporate change. My belief system of working hard and striving to always do a good job, along with the continual learning and development opportunities, fit my MO. There was always some task to master and forth I went... to master.

The company I worked for was California-based so the mindset was progressive and consistently on the edge of new and better ways to do business. In my division, each contributor was seen as a functional expert and there was an attitude of "You see a problem? Go ahead and fix it." Collaboration with various business groups and stakeholders was standard protocol as we sought win-win-win solutions. My desire to be part of something bigger was easily fed as a variety of different high-level project and system integrations always seemed to be on the table.

My bi-coastal team was responsible for approximately 45% of the two billion dollar world-wide accounts receivable portfolio, ranging from multi-million dollar distributor accounts to individual annual software purchases. We were a lean but not a very mean bunch, working hard to engage positively with both internal and external customers. My immediate team was split between the east and the west coast, elongating my normal business hours to an average of 65 hours per week. My team was fantastic and super to work with, dedicated to not just meeting but exceeding the extraordinary financial goals and business objectives set forth.

I truly enjoyed the interactions with my peers as well as expanding my connections to go beyond the small homogeneous state of New Hampshire. With customers spread throughout the Americas, as well as with headquarters in California, I made the best of the travel opportunities, always trying to fit in a few extra days for exploration of areas I might not otherwise have the opportunity to visit. One year we even had our global team meeting in Austria... a convenient way to check climbing the Matterhorn off the list.

While I was excited to tackle the demands of the day and take action on the larger, longer-term goals, eventually the constant use of high energy turned feelings of flow and mastery to depletion and dread. Without sufficient breaks to balance my inner resources and reserves, stress and the pressure of so much to manage drip-drip-dripped me towards burnout. The key word here is sufficient. Even though I took time to go on retreat, hike my stress away in the mountains, and treat myself to the occasional massage, these were temporary fixes for a bucket that was leaking and now breaking at the seams. At first, the energy of stress and all that adrenaline is the glue that keeps things going. Glue is only a temporary fix, though, and you can't use it to repair things for very long.

The problem with excessive stress leading to burnout is that you don't usually notice it until it plops itself onto your lap, especially if you're a go-getter and task-master. The go-go-go is so fast it has you missing the obvious markers. Progressive adaptation to the constant speed of things makes it hard to know how far away from calm and ease you've gotten... until there's something that shakes you to compare and become aware. For some, this might be when a loved one receives a diagnosis or suddenly passes. For others, it might be a car accident or injury that has you incapacitated for a time. For others still, it might be the realization that you feel 200 pounds lighter after a two week vacation. For me, it came from my then six-year-old.

Did I mention that, besides this thrilling, yet secretly threatening, corporate position, I was also a single parent of three growing boys... with two different fathers and all the complexity that came with that? I also had a big old beautiful 1891 Victorian house, a big child of sorts that needed a variety of minor repairs and major renovations. Yes, more wonderful pieces of my puzzle and the main reasons why I felt the need to "make it".

I wanted to be a good provider. I wanted to have a safe, secure, and loving home for my amazing boys to enjoy. I wanted to be a great example to them - that you could do anything with hard work and dedication. Coming from a history where I never felt I was good enough, I wanted to prove to myself that I was capable and able. As a professional woman and mother in America, shouldn't I be able to do it all? With my fundamental mindset of independence and self-reliance, my immediate answer was "of course". I thought I had enough tenacity, drive, and grit to be all things to all people. If I was amazing enough to create these beautiful lives, how could I not take care of everything that came with it? Plus, relying on anyone else to do what needed to be done, after my life's journey to this point, wasn't even a consideration.

On any given early evening, you could find me tapping away at home on my laptop, catching up with the late-day California requests or conference calls. After picking up the kids from school and other activities, I'd connect to the office before dinner so I could feel comfortable in blocking at least a few hours with my kids before the end of their day. After they were snug in bed or settled for the night, more screen time. "If I can get to it now while it's fresh, tomorrow will be an easier day." I had bought into this whacked-out belief system of forth-coming balance. I can be so silly.

Although I don't remember what I was wearing, I do remember the position of my desk against the dining room wall, sun low but streaming in from the window to offer a gentle light on the papers strewn about. I still had my headset on my head from the conference call I just finished, my mind engrossed in some finance approval request.

Connor, my youngest, came over to me and said "Mommy, you don't need to worry about coming to my event at school tonight. I know you have a lot of work to do so it's okay for you not to come."

What???

He repeated himself.

The blood drained out of me and I nearly threw up.

What had I been doing?!? Everything in me sank. This little six-year-old already knew more about my life than I did. He knew where I'd been placing my priorities and it certainly wasn't on him or his brothers. For all he knew, they were placeholders of quality time when Mommy got around to it. And, being the big heart that he is, he was selflessly already giving me an out. Ouch!

My wake up call.

Unfortunately my wake up call hadn't been the constant tightness and tension in my neck, as hard and impenetrable as concrete. My wake up call hadn't been the pressure in my chest that I felt whenever I really stopped to check. My wake up call hadn't been the carpal tunnel that had aggravated itself to the point where custom-fit braces for both hands were necessary for me to work through the day. My wake up call hadn't been the intense cluster headaches I occasionally got, feeling as if a spear had been driven into my skull through my eye socket, or the more frequent bloody noses that came out of nowhere. My wake up call hadn't been the inability to have a 50 hour work week be a realistic possibility. My wake up call hadn't been any of these because I had acclimated, driving myself forth and thinking this was just the way it was.

Sure, I'd been trying to slow down and take specific breaks away from work, changing my focus onto something that gave me a mental break and breathing room. I had been practicing yoga for a number of years now (even doing teacher training), going off on retreats or nature exploration trips on the weekends when I didn't have the boys, reading lots of affirming and spiritual books, and quieting myself with meditation when I could. Every other Sunday night when the boys were at their dads I had a ritual of making myself a special meal and treating myself to a candlelit dinner.

I would also spend time organizing the house so my environment was clean and uncluttered, get my hands in the dirt with various landscaping projects, and encouraging my creative side to guide decorative and restorative projects around the house. There was a deep sense of accomplishment in taking care of our home. It was a safe resting place.

But it wasn't enough. There was too much pulling at me on the other side. How was it ever going to change? (I wish I knew then what I know now.)

So right then and there, with six-year-old Connor's innocent statement slamming me like a 2X4, I knew I had to make some changes. There's no way I wanted to be *that* parent, the one who went through the motions of care but wasn't really taking care. I knew it hadn't always been like this but, wow, where it had gotten to?! It was bad enough that I still felt lots of guilt and sadness that the whole dual-parent family structure had dissolved... on two occasions. No job was going to take the place of my kids and having a connected life with them. Hopefully I could figure it out soon so it wasn't too late.

Connor's wake up call also gave me the chance to not only review how was I showing up as a parent but how was I showing up as a person. How happy was I really? What was feeding my soul? How often did I really smile - without my favorite sarcasm attached? I started noticing the level and depth of my walking impatience, narrowness of view, short-temperedness, tightness in body, and lingering frustration over little things that didn't matter. The excitement of Monday, my favorite workday, evaporated like water in hot sun and shifted to depleting my energy reserves. Inside I was flailing and needed to get out before I started failing... even more than I already was.

If anything was to change, I needed to take purposeful, corrective action so I could be more balanced in my work and life. I started shutting my laptop off early when I had the boys, creating space for elongated family time. I moved some of my Accounts Receivable portfolio off my plate (did I mention that, besides my management responsibilities, I also had my own portfolio of high-profile accounts?). I did my best to consolidate and delegate other activities, create personal boundaries around my time, and maintain 55 hours per week. To be honest, I never mastered it all for very long. Personal and professional expectations and work ethic habits had been formed. My own doing.

Eventually, I decided I had had enough. My adrenals were exhausted, no longer able to keep the excitatory stress energy going that had previously carried me through the non-stop day. I had spiraled into burnout and didn't see any fun or excitement in what I was doing anymore.

Looking for a different position within the larger organization seemed like it would only switch the content of my work product so I took that option off the table. Getting another job with another company was also furthest in thought for me. It would mean jumping into a new fire and starting over from scratch. Sorry, but I wasn't going to do that, at least not right away.

There was a lot to ponder. On the one hand was the desire for financial security and being able to support my family. On the other hand was really caring for my family and honoring my life. I felt like my back was against the wall with this mess I had created and I didn't see much of an option at that time besides leaving. Plus, to be honest, I felt too tired to figure out any other way (I wish I had my current me on my side then) and, once I made up my mind, that seemed to be the only answer I could see. So there I went... diving off a cliff.

Skip ahead to the present and I'm in a very different place. I wake up every morning and decide what I'm going to do with it. There's purposeful space and room to breathe in my day, to get plenty of exercise, feed my body good food, and take care of myself in whatever way that means. Sure, I have a busy calendar and priorities on my list, but I don't feel pressured or choked by them. I can slow down enough to actively choose how I'll attend to the day's events with deliberate intention and discernment.

Professionally, I'm on the other side of the desk... literally. Instead of me being the compressed and stressed business professional trying to figure out how to make it all work, I'm now the relief system, coaching those task-mastered comrades as they turn in their stress badge, not their employment badge. I'm that person I wish I had as I was maneuvering through those last set of years, someone who would've been instrumental in helping me stay anchored to my personal and professional goals and balance points, to remain clear about what was truly important, to help me integrate stress management techniques that were simple and effective, and to put it all into real-life practice so I could live with greater harmony and ease.

I feel extremely fortunate to have built a life around my passions and purpose, grateful every day for the challenges, pain points, and muck that I had to wade through to be here. Weaving my educational background in psychology and consciousness studies, my professional career in finance and management, my deeply centered life in mindfulness, all my professional trainings and certifications (dozens... I'm a life-long learner), I'm constantly inspired to share valuable practices and insights of personal empowerment and authentic living. So far I've reached over 20,000 people - not a point of brag but a reflection of the extent and vitality of my heart passion and purpose.

While the journey hasn't always been easy, I do know that the heart never leads you astray. Along this way, I've learned more about myself than I initially cared to, released old belief systems that were keeping me shattered and battered, and grew to finally really deeply care and love myself. I feel empowered in the decisions I make for my life every single day and I'm in charge. And while I don't always like it, what happens to me is my doing. If it's a shit storm, I've been helping to make that happen. If it's awesome sauce with flow and ease, I've been helping to make that happen. I've learned that taking ownership of my life doesn't have to be as hard and complicated as I thought it would be. I also know that I don't need to wait for hard lessons to knock me around in order to create change. Something new and different is available right here and now. It's my choice.

I want you to feel like you have choice as well. You don't need to keep saying "Yes" to everything, forgetting that healthy boundaries of "No" or "Not now" are also a "Yes". You don't need to wait until your kids graduate college to make that heart-desired move (new job, different location, divorce, travel, going back to school). You don't need to wait until your body implodes or your mind explodes to take action on what you need. You don't need to leave your life to keep your life.

I share my corporate story as a reflection of what you don't need to do. Learn from my choices, both skillful and unskillful. I'm here to offer hope that life can be beautiful in many ways, all without leaving your job or your family, and without reactive decisions that trajectory your future to scary unknown places.

Everyday Ease: Mindfully Moving From Burnout To Balance is your first step in getting to know your beautiful self again. While deceptively simple and easy, it will guide you to loving yourself strong from the inside out, feeding you with personal empowerment and sustaining confidence. As you become your priority, you'll be inspired to continue looking inside with gratitude and joy, happy to be choosing a path without regret or harm. Reflected in a favorite quote by Diane von Furstenberg:

When a woman becomes her own best friend,
life becomes easier.

Let's do this!

With lots and lots of Peace and Love,
Shanti

2

WHAT'S YOUR WHY?

Ease is the sign of grace in everything.
~ Marty Rubin ~

When you say the words "everyday ease", what comes to mind?

Perhaps a cock-eyed, quizzical expression or look of confusion pops onto your face since you haven't felt ease in decades. "I have no idea" might be an instantaneous thought. Or perhaps you took a deep breath and instantly transported yourself to a tropical island in the Caribbean... blue water, sparkly ocean sand, the sun shimmering on your body, and any sense of responsibility nowhere to be found.

Imagine it, though. What would ease look like if you had it in your life on a regular basis? What would it feel like, smell like, taste like? How would you spend your time? What clothes would you wear? What words would you use to greet the world? Who would you choose to have in your life and how would your relationships be? Close your eyes for a moment and let "ease" flow into your consciousness. Drift away into the possibilities. This is how you tap into making them real.

Imagine yourself…
Embodied in the energy of ease.
Close your eyes… what do you see?
Connect with your body… what do you feel?
Tap into your heart… what does it say?

If your body connects with this sense of everyday ease, you may notice an automatic depth to your breath or a sigh of relief that genuinely settles any tension. Wonderful. Do that on purpose now. Take a nice deep breath in… and now let it out with a big long *Aaahhhh*, doing that a few more times. Go ahead. No one's watching and, if they are, super fantastic! Perhaps they'll join you in decompressing for a few moments.

Some words, feelings, and experiences that might come to mind when you connect with the energy of ease:

- ✓ A sense of grounding
- ✓ Balance and steadiness
- ✓ Relaxation
- ✓ Peace and calm
- ✓ Clarity of thought
- ✓ Feeling great in your body with energy for the whole day
- ✓ Having space and time to get quiet and not feeling rushed
- ✓ Easily living your passion and purpose

✓ Taking the time to listen to another

✓ Opening your heart in a compassionate way

✓ Letting go of the judging and criticizing mind

✓ A deep knowing of what's really important

✓ Being connected and in synch with the natural flow of life

If you had ease in your life everyday,
what would that mean for you?
How would things be different?
What would open up and, conversely,
what could you let go of?

Take a few minutes to do this now. Really. I know it's easy to just read the words and skim over the action request but that's not going to get you connected to what you really want and how you really want to feel. Skimming like that is what happens in all the busyness, glossing over the essence of what's there. So go back, take a few moments, re-read the above words and imagine. Let your whole Being begin to awaken to the possibilities that exist for you.

What did you discover? How did the vision of your life appear with this full feeling of ease? What exciting possibilities popped up and came into awareness? Jot some of those down so you can come back to them and remind yourself later on.

_____

_____

Know that activating your thoughts through the authentic feeling sense of ease begins lining up the world of creation. When you connect to the energy of what you want, things somehow start to fall into place. The Universe conspires with you and you organically move from the intangible to the tangible without driving yourself hard or depleting your energy resources.

With everyday ease, the irritations, agitations, and frustrations that usually poke your stress buttons are no longer bothersome. With a clear head, you can see situations for what they are and are able to decide what you want to do about them. *You* are in control - not them. And for those bigger issues, well, they may still be big but your reactions aren't. You're much better at putting things into perspective because you're grounded and balanced with ease as your root.

Be your beautiful self.
Let your Light shine near and far.
There is only one of you.
What a gift you are!

What's Your Why?

Why are you not only interested in creating greater ease in your life but taking the important actions steps of engaging with this material and message?

Perhaps you're at a breaking point, where people and events are falling apart left and right and you don't have the energy to pick up the pieces. Perhaps you're noticing yourself yelling at your kids or fighting with your partner over the smallest of details. Perhaps that fighting has resulted in a separation or divorce or you're transfixed in an unfulfilling or demeaning partnership. Perhaps you're partaking in the care of your parents, trying to love them as best you can but feeling like there's not enough of you to go around and secretly resenting this additional caregiving role.

Perhaps the demands of work are so constant that taking a break doesn't seem worth it and camaraderie fades as you too often reject offers to go out to lunch. Perhaps you want to scream "Stop interrupting me!" at the next person that asks "Got a minute?" Perhaps your mind is so busy reviewing your never-ending to-do list that you miss key points being shared in meetings.

Perhaps the tension in your neck is so tight that it would take a jackhammer to break up the feeling of concrete that has set in. Perhaps you're feeling ragged and whipped around by all the things and people you need to attend to, prickly at the thought of being around people, and just want to crawl in bed and hide... or run away. Perhaps you haven't gotten a good night's sleep since before the oldest was born, accustomed to the lackluster energy you have with the meager five hours of sleep. Perhaps you hold your breath without realizing it and breathe so shallowly that it's hard to catch your breath walking up a few flights of stairs. Perhaps it's been so long since you've had fun and hysterically laughed out loud that you wouldn't recognize yourself in that moment.

Perhaps you've given up on ever getting back into shape and feeling comfortable and confident in your skin. Perhaps your tight fitting clothes are only a reflection of a worn-out ensemble and self-care that's waiting its turn. Perhaps emotionally eating or drinking is a best friend. Perhaps sex with your partner is measured in months or years and not days. Perhaps your body is starting to show signs of stress wear and tear, moving past the occasional ache into chronic illness or consistent pain.

Perhaps the rat race is the only element that's keeping it all together and you think that, if you stop, it'll all fall apart.

There are lots of reasons why you've come to this place and, no matter what you find, it's OK. The important point is that you're here and ready to take some action. Take a few minutes now to reflect on and **write down your list of "Whys"** below; those things that have pushed you to this place, those things that you'd like to change and be different. And after you've gotten your short list written, spend a few more minutes going deeper. Tap into the needs that are underneath. There's usually a lot more waiting to be discovered.

_____

_____

_____

_____

_____

_____

_____

While that reflective exercise may have started out with the obvious hassles and energy drains, perhaps you also tapped into some of your basic needs that aren't being met right now or discovered underlying issues you weren't aware of before. Some needs that may be present for you:

- ✓ A sense of worth and value
- ✓ Feeling important to others
- ✓ Desiring unconditional love
- ✓ Physical, emotional, relational safety
- ✓ Support that comes easily and without the need to request
- ✓ Financial freedom and security
- ✓ Being heard and understood when you share yourself with others
- ✓ Being accepted by others for who and how you are
- ✓ Space and time for you to be yourself
- ✓ Shared responsibility in the house
- ✓ A body that feels free and alive, connected to the healthy food you eat

Identifying these unmet needs and challenges is super important as you begin this personal journey of creating a life that's more fulfilling. Without knowing what the driving forces are behind your perceptions and how you're relating to the world, you can't take proper corrective action towards creating true harmony and ease. As you play with this Easebook, the needs you have that are unfulfilled will move closer towards fulfillment and the intensity of challenges should lessen or disappear altogether. With gentleness, patience, and love, everything can shift.

3

MINDFULNESS: FOUNDATION OF EASE

Smile, breathe, and go slowly.
~ Thich Nhat Hanh ~

In case no one's told you lately, you're amazing. You're fantabulous, beautiful, fascinating, and completely awesome! Truly. Have you forgotten that? Did the world get so busy on you that you've lost this recognition of yourself?

If you sigh-fully answered "Yes", I totally get that. I've been there myself so don't worry. You're here now and this Easebook is your oxygen mask. Just like in an airplane when it's experiencing lots of turbulence, you have to put the oxygen on *you* first, before anyone else (even your super amazing kids). If you don't have oxygen to breathe, nothing in life is possible. As it is, you breathe life into so many others in so many ways… and they don't even know the half of it.

This Easebook is your everyday reminder to breathe this oxygen and freshness into your life, to be present and loving to yourself no matter what, to guiltlessly give yourself a little bit of space that's just yours, and to help you slow down enough to notice that there's an amazingly beautiful Being behind all that doing. And, by the way, this book is purposefully called an Easebook instead of a workbook because, honestly, you've got enough work on your plate. The invitation, then, is to put down the pressure to do (it's never-ending anyways) and come into a sweet, loving, affirming, and deeply connected relationship with your beautiful Being. This Easebook will help you do this, staying focused and on course to have your best self be what guides your day.

Let's play for a minute and start this ease with some breath right now, letting freshness and spaciousness fill your body and mind. You'll do this often so there's no better time than right now to get used to it. Sit for a moment, letting yourself rest on your seat, fully supported by the chair or cushion, and place a hand gently on your heart or chest area.

Breathe into your body.
Breathe into your heart.
Breathe into this moment.
Invite yourself to simply Be.

Stay here for a bit and notice the shift that this pause into presence offers. Did a little bit of grace and ease show up, a little bit of letting go happen? What shifted in your body and the sensations there? Did the mind slow down, even just a smidgeon, enough for a spontaneous sigh of relief to enter the space?

Ease begins with this type of presence: a presence that has you pausing to connect to yourself in the present moment, to take a momentary break from the thousand miles per hour speed of your life, and to notice what's there. It's the beginning stage of taking care of and loving yourself more deeply… which is the oxygen that helps you take care of everything that's important in your world. Without this pausing into presence, it's impossible to create ease. You're simply moving too fast.

The presence from which this Easebook is being offered is called mindfulness.

Mindfulness is being tuned in with awareness of your present moment as it exists, both inside and outside of you, in a way that doesn't judge and offers acceptance of what is.

The typical mind wants to make perfect sense of everything. It categorizes and labels, takes sides, judges as right or wrong, and reacts without true cause. Its view is narrow, determined, and, while focused, is focused in a way that inhibits possibilities and has you getting stuck in wrong perceptions… leading to a whole mess of trouble.

Mindfulness changes all of that by dropping fixated assumptions and judgments in favor of curiosity and interest. By slowing down, being curious, and observing more deeply, a more cohesive and expanded relationship with what exists right now forms. There's greater opportunity to recognize emotions and feelings, understand their causes and conditions, and make more skillful decisions that are connected to what's truly needed. With mindfulness' eye of understanding, you're more fully informed about and accepting of what is, helping you to be kinder, more appreciative, accepting, compassionate, and connected to the larger shared humanity.

Mindfulness Hand

I liken mindfulness to a hand with the palm open and fingers gently spread. Whatever's alive in the present moment drops onto the palm, offering a moment to notice what's there with the vast myriad of differing conditions.

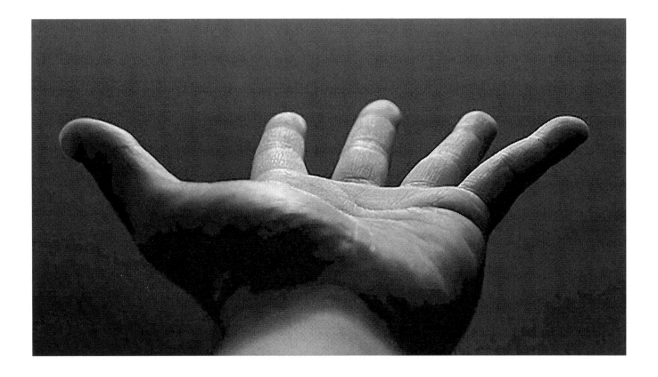

Take a moment now to stop and pause. Close your eyes if you'd like so you can tune inward without the distraction of things around you. Connect to your breathing, feeling it arrive and release in your body. If it feels right, place a hand on your chest or belly and notice yourself in this moment. Keep breathing and connecting to the breath and your body. Settle in for a minute or two then ask yourself how you feel. Check in with these reflective questions:

* *What's happening with my breath and my body?*
* *How am I feeling and what emotions are alive for me right now, including the ones that are running around in the background behind the bigger and more obvious stuff?*
* *What words and tone of voice are being scripted in my head?*
* *In what direction is my mind pointed and what is it focusing on?*
* *What's my overall experience right now?*

You may have noticed a shortness or holding of your breath, slight tightness in the chest built up from the compressed schedule of the day, or a dull headache lingering underneath a layer of dehydration. Perhaps your mind is dwelling on the recent disagreement you had with your partner, still not feeling seen or heard. Your head might be feeling depleted and full from all of today's thinking. Perhaps there's a desire to move and do something, an energy of feeling unsettled or "buzzing". A craving for something sweet or crunchy may be waiting to be satisfied.

Whatever you discover, welcome it all as valuable information, even if it's an attitude of annoyance or a chronic pain in your body. All of this has been impacting your present moment experience anyways so it's best to know what your conditions are like. How can you take care of yourself well if you don't know what's really there? How can you take appropriate action if there are important pieces of information missing?

Know that what you discover might not always be pleasant, particularly when you deal with matters of the mind. If you're any type of human, you can get pretty judgmental about things and people, especially yourself. Being your worst critic is a torture system your ancient brain came up with to keep you safe and to improve your condition by reminding you (loudly and unskillfully sometimes) what *not* to do. Positive reinforcement is not it's organic forte. And you don't just experience these judgments once as a fleeting thought. You can spend hours, even days, ruminating over events that have long ago passed. Connected to these judgments and criticisms are draining emotions: sadness, anger, pity, jealousy, low self-esteem, lack of confidence, blame, shame, guilt, remorse, dread, anxiety... the list seems endless. These emotions disconnect you from your higher and more positive energies and from keeping top of mind how awesome you really are. They keep you small, constricted, and closed off from living in greater ease.

Mindfulness is going to breathe new life into all of this. By slowing to know what's alive for you in the present moment, you have the chance to understand it better. When you understand it better, more effective and beneficial solutions appear, and next best steps seem to be right at your fingertips. You're less caught up in the emotion of a problem and can step back to observe, reflect, understand, analyze, and choose.

* *What's the need that's calling to me and seeking my attention?*
* *How can I take care of myself amidst everything else that's going on in this moment?*
* *What would make the next moment more appropriate or beneficial?*

The pausing and checking in aspects of mindfulness are, of course, counter to what typically happens as you attempt to task-master the day. *"I don't have time to pause and check in. I'm too busy. I'll never get anything done that way!"* While it might seem like that, realistically, that's like saying *"I don't have time to know if the tools I'm using for this problem are the right ones. I'll just grab whatever's closest and easiest. Fingers crossed."* You'd never do business like that so why apply the same crazy methodology to your life?

Slow to Know

With the palm open and fingers gently spread, not much is caught. Life flows and moves through so the next moment can land, flow, and move. *"What's here now... and now?"* With mindfulness, you're not grabbing ahold of what's there and trying to make it stay or go away. Staying would be having the palm cupped and fingers closed so that you can hold onto what you really like (dark chocolate or sleeping extra late). Pushing away your experience would be closing the hand to make a fist or a hand straight out in rejection (liver and onions or having a meeting with your colleague Joe who annoys you as he constantly clears his throat). Grasping, attaching, or craving. Denying, disassociating, or dismissing.

Wanting more of what you like and less of what you don't like in a discerning and aware way is fantastic but typically the level of like or dislike employed as you meet the moments of the day are reactionary with little consciousness involved. Perceptual habits can be strong and forceful, distort reality, or reject what is, all without great effort on your part. Not being satisfied with what's there, the desire is to change your circumstance so that it's more to your liking and fits in your world better. When everything lines up, neat and tidy, the world feels wonderful. When you're in control, life is good. Unfortunately, this is not the case most of the time - it's not lined up perfectly and you can't control it - so dissatisfaction, disagreement, and unhappiness are attitudes that can quickly appear.

This resistance to what is causes a lot of unnecessary stress and suffering, creating even more chaos and dis-ease as you try to untangle yourself and get to a place of ease and contentment. Stress, more than anything else, is the biggest source of energy depletion in life, rooted in how events and circumstances are viewed and the desire to have them be different than they are.

Stop for a moment and think about any situation or person that causes you frustration, irritation, worry, or any emotion that feeds negativity. Why is this such a pain point? What's causing that emotion of unease? It's because you want it to be different than it is. There's something about it that isn't fitting with your idea of how it should be or how you want it to be. So how to get control over your experiences?

Mindfulness is the pathway to the control you seek.

Let me clarify. It's not that you're going to get your way with mindfulness, that people and things will suddenly line up in order to fulfill your ever-wanting needs and desires. While it might be super cool to have this incredible power of control, I'm not sure you'd really want to be in charge that much. It's an awful lot of responsibility to be at the helm of what other people do and, basically, you're messing with the natural flow of things. Plus, to be honest, even though you're super smart and perceptive, you don't know everything. There's a back-story to most things. There are so many interconnected details to any given situation, you don't want to use your power of assumption to decide. You know how *that* usually turns out.

Instead, mindfulness gives you control... over you. Instead of rejecting your situation and getting frustrated with it (insert whatever emotion might be applicable), there's a level of acceptance that comes with mindfulness. You're accepting that this is what your moment is. This acceptance doesn't mean that you agree with it but you do accept that this is what is. If it's a frustrating moment, you identify and recognize that it's a frustrating moment. If it's a happy moment, you identify and recognize that it's a happy moment. Again, acceptance doesn't mean agreement; it just means that you're aware and acknowledging that whatever is is.

This level of acceptance gives you the power to settle yourself in the moment. Instead of wrestling and fighting with it, you're right there, face to face. The opportunity now exists for you to get curious, look more deeply, see more clearly, and come to a better understanding of the situation. This awareness and acceptance make up the perceptual framework that gives you the power to work with your mind and decide what you're going to feel, think, and do about any situation. *"That sweater is so ugly. What was she thinking?"* might change to *"Interesting color combination. She's got a creative mind."* You decide that you don't want to be so critical and judgmental and instead want to feel kind or curious. It's your choice. Same situation. Different response and feeling.

Practice doesn't make perfect.
Practice reduces the imperfection.
~ Toba Beta ~

This type of engagement with life takes practice... lots of practice (and super for you being here in this practice zone). It's counter to the speed-demon habits that control so many of your actions and reactions throughout any given day, happening so fast that they blur into the continuum of experiences and go unnoticed.

Have you ever had a situation where you wondered *"How did I get here? How did this happen?"* I'm sure more than you'd like. If you break it down to look back at everything that led to the "what the heck" situation, you'll start to see a stream of decision-points that could have turned things around to be very different if you had been more aware of them. Deciding to be the master *of* life, versus being mastered *by* life, requires effort and diligence. Tenacity is needed to awaken consciousness enough to change the status quo and reprogram the automatic defaults of perception and action.

Out of habit, when you come into contact with something or someone, the brain works faster than lightning speed to make sense of it and put it into a perspective that you can easily understand. It categorizes this contact as either good (*"I like it. This is the best thing ever. Give me more."*), bad (*"I can't stand it. It's ugly, I don't want it. Please make it go away."*), or neutral (*"Oh, was there something there? I didn't even notice. Too bland for me."*). With so much stimuli hitting your perceptual field and senses all day (the brain processes 40 billion bits every second but you only process about 50 of those), there's a part of you that needs this categorization so that life will be easier and more manageable. Your brain makes decisions based on accumulated knowledge and prior experiences, immediately assessing a situation so you don't have to waste a ton of energy going through a whole analysis process. It would be pretty cumbersome and energetically expensive to start figuring out all your likes and dislikes from scratch.

While this auto-processing may seem like it's making life easier and less cumbersome, it has the effect of coloring your view, making it harder to see what's actually there. Your views are filled with biases and assumptions. For instance, the love you have for your daughter overshadows your assessment of the impact her snide and sarcastic remarks have on her younger brother. Your colleague Joe irritates you so you're inadvertently less inclined to ask for his feedback in meetings. You probably don't notice these subtle biases of view but they do make a difference in how you relate to the experience at hand.

With mindfulness, you have a chance to get to know your habits better, to pause and check in to see what might actually be true with your perceptions and belief systems. With curiosity and interest in knowing what's really contained in your experience, you ask open-ended questions such as:

* *What's here that I might not know? What other possibilities exist?*
* *How am I reacting to the situation… in my body, mind, emotions?*
* *What are my beliefs around this situation or this person? Do I know them to be currently true or are they tied to a past experience?*
* *What's here that I'm not noticing because I want to believe what I've always believed?*
* *Is there anything I'm disguising, glossing over, or seeing through filtered lenses?*
* *What is motivating me in this moment? What would I really like instead?*
* *How can I make this a better or more appropriate moment?*
* *How can I take care of my anger / sadness / worry / frustration / _____ and not cause further harm or suffering?*

Notice that all of these questions are generous with interest, curiosity, kindness, self-care, and an honest desire to know. You aren't accusing yourself or telling yourself you're bad or wrong that you have a certain view. Instead, you're coming to know what your current view is. There's a sincere interest in learning more about yourself and your situation, in a way that maintains positivity and self-respect. Taking care in this way has you taking action that doesn't cause harm, helping you to flourish and honor your heart-based intentions. This is the beginning stage of dismantling stress and increasing resiliency.

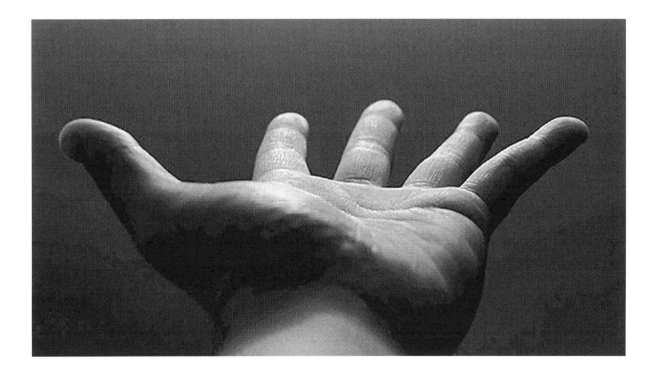

Mindfulness as open palm and fingers gets you to the who, what, why, where, and how of You in a way that has you generating more understanding, acceptance, and self-compassion than you've ever experienced before. Because you're not overshadowing yourself with how you think you should be but are instead being real, you can love yourself more deeply and honestly, even the quirky parts. By frequently pausing to check in and ask *"What's here for me?"*, you're less inclined to live out of habit and more inclined to actively decide what you want to bring to the moment of now. You get to choose and be in control. A pretty powerful way to add resiliency and look at the circumstances related to burnout, wouldn't you agree?

> *Breathe into your body.*
> *Breathe into your heart.*
> *Breathe into this moment.*
> *Invite yourself to simply Be.*

Reality Check

To clarify any potential confusion, mindfulness is not all peace and calm nor does it make everything right. Granted, when you understand your moment and take care of it and yourself as best you can, you're more likely to generate peace and calm but that's a by-product. Mindfulness is, in actuality, a reality check.

If you're frustrated, you get real with yourself about that frustration. You feel the sensations of frustration in your body (heat in the neck, hands slightly clenched). You notice what's going on in your mind (the rambling dialogue of dissatisfaction with a tone that's sharp). You may become aware of an urge to take action and voice your opinion, simultaneously countered by your "professional" voice telling you it's not worth it and to just let it go.

Palm open, frustration lands. No judgment or rejection; not labeling as right or wrong. "*Frustration is here right now*" is the acknowledgement, and instead of unknowingly spewing that frustration out onto whomever is closest (watch out co-worker) or stuffing it inside (more crunchy food please), with mindfulness, your experience might look more like this:

"I'm feeling pretty upset right now. I can feel my blood pressure rising, heat in my chest and head, this urge to say something I know isn't helpful. Hmmm... how can I take care of myself? I can breathe and calm my energies down. I can get up and take a walk. Perhaps I'll practice patience or kindness. Let me reframe my mind to what's working well here. Perhaps I might see the other person as also right, although, to be honest, I'm not there yet."

And while you're able to be a better witness and observe yourself more completely with the eyes of mindfulness, it isn't a matter of just letting your life happen with you standing back and not participating. Rather, since you're more tuned in and aware, there's a sense of aliveness and deeper connection to what you need. You're a unique, exciting, fascinating, and interesting Being. Mindfulness will bring acceptance and wonder to all of that.

Another fantastic benefit of mindfulness is that it can help you get clear on situations and circumstances that lead to unpleasantness and drain your energy on a regular basis. For instance, if you find that most afternoons feel chaotic and taxing, you might consider changing your activity schedule around, shortening the period of time that you'll give attention to something, or consciously taking breaks throughout the day. When you take care of yourself in this way, you end up being less stressed, more productive and efficient, and much more satisfied with the day. Mindfulness is a health promoting practice, one of deep self-care and love.

Mindfulness will also help you create a different relationship with those parts of yourself that you don't particularly like or find to be difficult. Remember that busy inner critic? Mindfulness is the beginning of changing that inner voice to one of support and kindness. Like being held in the arms of a loving mother, your suffering is attended to with care, generosity, and heart-felt compassion. There's deep healing in this special type of self-love.

Why is all of this so important? You're a caring and loving person that's always doing your best. It pains you when you aren't able to meet the standards you've set, you don't have the amount of energy you'd like to give your loved ones or favorite projects, or you feel like you're just riding the surface of life. You want to be engaged and fully present with your experiences, show up with energy and vitality, and have your heart's shine lead whatever you're doing. You want to have fun, laugh and express yourself freely, have a body that moves with ease and confidence, and have a mind that's your best friend. You want contentment, satisfaction, and happiness to be the day's backdrop.

~~~~~~~~~~~~~~~~~~~~~~~~~~~~~~~~~~~

What else would you add to this?

~~~~~~~~~~~~~~~~~~~~~~~~~~~~~~~~~~

*It would be super amazing to have **more** of this in my life:*

_____

_____

_____

*It would be super amazing to have **less** of this in my life:*

_____

_____

_____

*I don't want to get to the end of my life and
find that I lived just the length of it.
I want to have lived the width of it as well.*

~ Diane Ackerman ~

4

TRAVELING WITH THE FABULOUS FRESH FIVE

The moment in between what you once were
and who you are now becoming
is where the dance of life really takes place.
~ Barbara De Angelis ~

You're about to embark on a journey back to where all of your systems - body, mind, spirit, energy - are connected and cohesive, where vitality and flow are seamless, and where you feel super spectacular on any given day for no particular reason.

With your mindfulness at the helm, you're going to navigate through some very important territory with the **Fabulous FRESH Five** aspects of health and well-being:

Food
Restful sleep
Exercise and movement
Stress management
Hydration

No doubt these are familiar to you but, just because they're familiar, doesn't mean they're always attended to. When the Fabulous FRESH Five are working well and in balance, everything else in life tends to be well and in balance. Sure, life still happens but you're better able to tackle the tough times and rebound with resiliency when the Fabulous FRESH Five are strong. That being said, however, when you're already busy trying to take care of so many things, it can feel overwhelming to add even one more thing onto your plate. Don't worry - as with everything else being offered in this Easebook, you'll take this journey at your own pace, one step at a time.

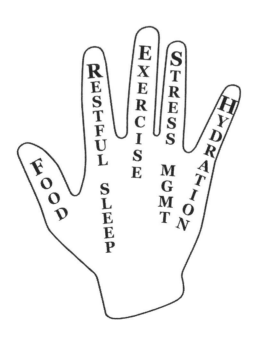

The Fabulous FRESH Five are like the five fingers on your hand. Everything is easier when you can use all five fingers to pick things up, put them down, and do what you need to do during the day. If one finger is broken, only minor adjustments need to be made in order to attend to the business at hand. If two or three fingers are broken, it gets harder to manage even the simplest of tasks without expending a lot of additional time and energy or calling in external supports. If four or five fingers are broken, the hand isn't very functional and certainly not able to do what it was designed to do. If this continued to be broken long-term, life would change significantly.

How balanced do you think you are in each of the Fabulous FRESH Five? Jot down your answers in the graph, knowing that, whatever you discover, it's good information from which to make changes or keep engaged with what positive things you're already doing. At the end of the Easebook's six weeks, you'll have a chance to reassess and see how things have shifted and changed.

On a scale of 1 - 10, with "1" being extremely poor and "10" being absolutely fantastic, rate each of the Fabulous FRESH Five:

FABULOUS FRESH FIVE	IN MY LIFE...	CURRENT RATE
Food	I eat clean and healthy food that naturally energizes my body. Meals are nutritionally balanced and in appropriate portion. I enjoy my food with minimal cravings. Sugar and processed foods are not common on my plate.	
Restful sleep	I regularly wake feeling rested and refreshed.	
Exercise & movement	I exercise my body every day for at least 30 minutes. I feel free, strong, capable, and physically fit, enjoying the movement of my body.	

STRESS **MANAGEMENT**	I have a positive outlook and I'm able to manage challenging situations in a constructive and appropriate way. I have a supportive community that cares for me.	
HYDRATION	I drink clean water through the day and am rarely thirsty.	

This Easebook is purposefully designed to offer many small adjustments that all lead to better self-care and internal harmony. The goal isn't to make things perfect. Most likely you're not going to land at a 10 for all Fabulous FRESH Five but, after "working the sheets" for six weeks, you'll see some good and steady improvements. If you've rated yourself 8 or above on any of the Fabulous FRESH Five, FANTASTIC!! Keep doing what you're doing. If you've rated 5 - 7, FANTASTIC! You're on your way. And if you've rated yourself 4 or below, FANTASTIC! This Easebook is the perfect venue to play with the different components of health and well-being, continually improving your rating as you incorporate the strategies and practices.

Shifting The Focus On You

I know it's not easy to switch gears, to all of a sudden start carving out time and space for your needs, to paying attention to you, but it's necessary if you want life to be more fulfilling and gratifying. Most likely your current state of affairs is that you've been chauffeuring family, work, home, and even community around for a very long time. And while you might be sitting in the driver's seat, you're most likely not the one calling the shots and directing where you're going. This Easebook is here to change all of that, not in a way that throws everyone else out of the car but one in which you are sitting in both the driver's and passenger's seat... with self-love reflecting back in the rear view mirror.

This Easebook is asking for a slight shift in focus. Instead of everyone and everything else being the highlight, you'll be actively inserting yourself into your time, attention, energy, mindset, and presence. You'll begin to strengthen personal boundaries that support yourself and causally support your world. You can do your best when you're at your best.

Breathe into your body.
Breathe into your heart.
Breathe into this moment of being,
Invite yourself to simply Be.

Travel Tips and Reminders

To keep your travels safe and with a positive mindset, here are some basic travel tips, guidelines, and reminders. Have them support your itinerary and pathway as you reach your destination.

Set Your GPS

If you've ever used a GPS (global positioning software) to travel, you know that one of the first things you need to do in order to get accurate directions is to enter your destination. Where do you want to go? Hopefully you're gaining clarity around that from what you've been writing and thinking about in the material above... improved health, kinder relationships, ease in your day, more defined personal boundaries and confidence in saying NO to others to say YES to yourself, the ability to ask for what you need, spaciousness to re-discover you, resiliency to stress and change, managing emotions in a loving way, confidence in your ability to meet your moments with a sense of composure, etc.

The next important thing after setting your destination in your GPS is to identify where you are right now. What's your starting point? If you don't have this set point, you can't possibly get accurate directions. You'll just keep going around and around in circles, down wrong roads and alleys, making costly and time consuming mistakes that have you feeling frustrated, tired, discouraged, and lost. For instance, if you want to spend more quality time with your family yet you're the Chair of three committees, you might be driving yourself in circles trying to find an exit route, creating a personal traffic jam.

Mindfulness is the "I am here" starting point that your whole GPS system relies upon so frequently checking in to where you are is important. The other cool thing about mindfulness is that, no matter how many travel mistakes you might make, you can always reset and start again in the present moment. Over the next six weeks of this Easebook, mindfulness will be your GPS. Keep coming back to where you are with awareness, interest, curiosity, kindness, heart-felt presence, and understanding. Make a plan from where you are.

Aspirations Light The Way

Any great journey always begins with heart-felt aspirations, excitement, and an intention to experience wonder and beauty. When you're joyfully anticipating what's ahead, the mind happily gets busy visualizing what it's going to be like, dreaming up all the places and things that will be experienced, and welcoming new memories. It's wonderful to have your future-state become a full-bodied present-state experience. With the mind-body-spirit senses onboard and ready to go, bumps in the road or detours that may slow your progress are somehow navigated around without a lot of effort. The bigger energy of YES and your determination to be successful somehow auto-correct travel challenges with perfect adjustments. Everything lines up with the light of empowered aspirations and inspirations.

So get inspired! Look back to the beginning of the book for how you answered "What would be possible?" in reflection of what it would look, feel, and seem like if ease were a bigger part of your life. What excites you about that change and the possibilities you imagined? Feel it in your bones so the connection to this possible and potential change becomes real. Imagine it as already existing. Jot down anything that's speaking to you here:

_____

_____

_____

Make It A Marathon

The journey of ease and self-care is a marathon, not a sprint. This can't be stressed enough! Just as the tortoise won the race, there's no gain if you go too fast and don't incorporate the activities and learn from the discoveries along the way. Ease doesn't come by rushing from one thing to another, checking it off on to-do list, or letting go of the things that are important for the sake of speed. Ease doesn't even happen by making it *the* goal, something that you're pursuing. It happens as a natural output of everything else you're doing to take care of You, making one decision at a time throughout the day.

    ✳ *Does this activity or thought add value or deplete my resources?*
    ✳ *What's the best thing for me in this moment?*
    ✳ *How can I stay grounded and keep a steady pace, recognizing the bigger goal but still staying in this moment taking this baby step?*

As you go through this Easebook, start wherever you are. Do what you can for the day and move on, being glad for what you've done, even if it was only one self-care activity. Perhaps tomorrow you'll be able to add one more, then one more, then one more. Perhaps your pace is adding one more thing every week. FANTASTIC! Do what you need to do to take care of yourself. Burnout comes when you try to pack it all in, doing more than you're realistically able to do. There's no competition here and no rush to get it all done. **Do what you can and leave the rest.** The pace of integration is slow and steady. With persistence and patience, gradually everything in this Easebook will make sense and you'll come to enjoy comprehensive self-care as a matter of habit and lifestyle. It's one purposeful step at a time.

Lift Off The Gas

All of the activities and reflections in this Easebook are connected to what's already happening in your life, presented in a way that tweaks a little bit of this and a little bit of that. If you feel pressure and stress to do everything at once, lift off the gas pedal and go a little slower. Stress is a good warning sign that you've gotten off course (it's probably one of the reasons why you're actually here) and will most likely have you running out of gas much sooner than you hoped or expected. You might also get discouraged and end up canceling the whole trip before you've given yourself a chance to even get going. There's plenty of time - no need to rush.

Keep On Keepin' On

Be gentle with yourself but don't give up on yourself. Change requires effort and diligence of time, energy, and attention. Personally commit to the material and activities being offered, making them non-negotiable. You're that important! Don't give up because you had a rough day, forgot to do a planned activity, or meandered off course because something else hijacked your attention or dragged you away. Begin again - from right here and now. Each step forward is a step in the right direction so reset your GPS and step back into your commitment without guilt, shame, or blame. And by the way, you're already ahead of the game and have created success by simply being here. You've recognized that you're important, worthy, deserving, and valuable. Awesome!

Play along. Be yourself. Have fun.

Change the Station

Do you have an inner critic that's constantly telling you how you didn't show up well enough, goes into an extreme and ruminating narrative about all the ways you aren't good enough, recalls with lightening speed every little mistake you've ever made since the beginning of time, keeps you feeling small and powerless, or has you fearing any new move since you'll "just mess this up, too!"? Welcome to the typical human mind.

While your inner critic may think it's doing you a favor by keeping you on task and out of harm's way, it's actually having the opposite effect. Has beating yourself up ever been a motivator that *really* worked, especially for the long haul? Have you ever made serious positive change under duress? Perhaps in extreme conditions that were part of a larger wake-up call like after having a heart attack or a near-fatal accident but, overall, change doesn't come about easily or lovingly from a root of negativity.

Instead, you feel motivated and inspired to move forward when you feel safe, secure, nourished, valued, empowered, excited, and worthy, when you're given positive attention and encouragement, and when you have a cheerleader on the sidelines rallying you and highlighting everything you're doing right. And while it's super important to have others that support your progress, realistically, the best person for this job is yourself.

The radio frequency of your mind is the voice you listen to more than any other. You listen to it when you're purposefully talking to yourself and also when it's behind the scenes like an unconscious tape recorder. You even listen to it when you're sleeping, usually playing itself out in your dreams. The messages of not being good enough are subtle and prevalent, leaving you feeling pretty bad and battering your self-esteem. As you travel these six weeks, the radio dial will be turned from Station Uckness to Station Awesomeness, filling you with positivity, care, kindness, gratitude, appreciation, acceptance, understanding, self-love, and compassion.

Get Back On Course With Affirmations

Affirmations are a fantastic way to turn the dial and switch away from the toxic messages that are replaying themselves over and over on Station Uckness. The perfect line-up of affirmations on Station Awesomeness can lift your spirit and get you grooving with excitement and joy by reminding you of what's working well in your life right now and adding hope and positivity for things to come. Choose one or two affirmations to take with you through the day or make up your own, repeating them like a song you can't get out of your head. It can be helpful to record your affirmation as a voice message on your phone or write it down on a beautiful piece of paper and place it where you'll see it often. Have the energy of the words invoke a feeling sense that's inspiring and moves through your body and mind as truth. Believe it and it is so.

- ✓ I completely love and accept myself just as I am right now.
- ✓ I'm doing the best that I can in this moment.
- ✓ I enjoy my successes, especially the small ones along the way.
- ✓ I love co-creating win-win-win situations.
- ✓ I am the change I wish to see in the world. It all begins with me.
- ✓ I am loving and deserving of love.
- ✓ Every cell in my body vibrates with health and positive energy.

41

- ✓ I nourish and nurture my body in healthy and loving ways.
- ✓ Everything is flowing and going to work out fine. I'm trusting the natural process of life.
- ✓ I work in a beautiful environment, perfect for me.
- ✓ My heart is open and I feel happy to be alive.
- ✓ I love sleeping well and waking up refreshed.
- ✓ My body is a beautiful expression of Spirit.
- ✓ I am kind and take care of myself well.

Amazing Discoveries Await You

Like an explorer seeing new sights for the first time, mindfulness and this Easebook will hopefully have curiosity be a mainstay for your day, seeing yourself through lenses of inquisitiveness, interest, and even humor. Laughter is a rare commodity for adults (kids easily laugh hundreds of times every day) so feel free to laugh at yourself and your circumstance any time it would feel right. Sometimes things can be so absurd that laughing at it is the best way to defuse tensions and lighten the stress load. Plus, in some moments it might be your only sane option.

Throughout the day, put out your Mindful Hand and notice "What's here?". The observational and curious lens of mindfulness will make it easier to connect the dots of how certain habits and reactions to regular everyday experiences affect other parts of your life. As you notice yourself in an openhearted and judgment-free way, instead or getting caught up in a sense of right and wrong or having the trouble spots manage your mood, your level of personal responsibility and ownership for your experience will increase. With this sense of empowerment comes less reactivity with more grace and ease.

You may begin to notice that you have a greater appreciation for all that you do and no longer beat yourself up for not meeting unrealistic expectations. As this attitudinal shift gets more deeply rooted, the reality of what's truly possible sets in and you start choosing more wisely, making decisions that offer you success: success in personal self-care, at home with family, in relationship with friends, and at work. You can see through the myriad of requests more easily and discernment of what's really important becomes your guide... and it makes you happy. With an empowered sense of self being at the hub, a new attitude takes hold: "What I do here and now matters... including how I'm taking care of me." Yeah!

As you get further into your journey, the importance of the Fabulous FRESH Five will start to click and you may begin to notice connections between what you ate, how you moved your body, and how you slept. You might become aware that clearer thinking and less reactivity happens when you eat healthy, exercise often, sleep well, and hydrate. Conversely, if you've had insomnia for three days you may notice zero patience, frequent emotional outbursts, and poor decision-making skills.

By integrating Peaceful Pauses, you may notice that this periodic break throughout the day eases the overall level of tension you feel and gives you a delicious amount of energy when you get home from the office (without caffeine or sugary sweets).

As you progress, you may notice a sense of organic ease and flow, an increase in even your casual presence, more patience, greater concentration for tasks at hand, and an overall increase in joy. Small things may make you smile without effort and many wonderful aspects of the day will begin to come alive. Bring all of these discoveries into your field of awareness and let them stay with you so that you feel saturated by their positivity.

Self-Love And Acceptance Are Fuel For The Long Haul

Whatever you discover as you journey through this Easebook, let it be held with the energy of love, kindness, and gratitude. Embrace it all, even those parts that you might not otherwise appreciate. If you discover habits that are no longer useful in your life, use them as fodder for growth and change, but don't reject the importance they once played in your life. It's just time to move on.

Loving yourself is the most important thing you can do in your life. Truly. Yes, I know you want success in so many areas but if self-love is overshadowed by the busyness of doing, it's all going to fall apart and burnout will take hold. Self-love is the foundation of any success. With the energy of mindfulness and love, your life will be a wonderful living dialogue and relationship. And don't forget that there's only one beautiful, amazing Being that is you. No matter the innumerable variety and diversity of elements available in creation, they will never be so perfectly aligned again to come up with someone like you. This is the one chance for you to Be so love yourself strong and let your Being shine!

Meditation As A Regular Rest Stop

Meditation is like a rest stop that finally shows up on the side of the road after you've been traveling for miles and miles. Taking this break in your trip, you have a chance to relieve yourself, stretch, refuel your vehicle, and check in with your mindful GPS and where you are. If there are any problems or unmet needs, you have the chance to address them before you get back on the road.

There are many styles and forms of meditation (too many to get into here), each with a slightly different affect. Over the past few decades, science has been validating many of the benefits of this ancient practice, supporting improvements in a whole range of aspects including productivity and focused attention, stress reduction, life satisfaction, emotional self-regulation, depression and anxiety, relational engagement, immune function, pain management, cardiovascular health, and compassion fatigue.

Meditation can also be a place of respite from which better decisions about everyday life can be made, offering a grateful place to settle down reactivity and all the unskillfulness that comes with that. When mind and body busyness are slowed, the heart has a chance to lead, intuition has a quiet space to be heard, and important insights are revealed. Some of the best ideas and "aha" moments come about in meditation.

While the instruction of meditation may be simple, it's not the easiest practice to develop, at least on your own. It's important to have the guidance of a skillful and knowledgeable teacher to build familiarity and awareness. As part of this Easebook journey, there are several guided meditations that can help enrich your life and integrate ease. To access, visit **http://bit.ly/EverydayEaseMeditations**. These meditations are yours so feel free to listen often as part of a formal practice of pausing or whenever you feel it would serve you best.

Setting aside some time every day to purposefully be present builds the muscle of ease and calm, increasing the level of resiliency you'll have to stress and change. A daily commitment of 15-20 minutes of meditative reprieve pays off in a grand way so enjoy the meditations and notice the benefits you receive both at that time and over time. Like many health care practices, meditation has a compounding effect that builds so engage often. You'll also be reminded periodically throughout the Easebook daily pages so play along, be yourself, have fun.

The Trip Never Ends

Like the "Song That Never Ends", the journey of your life also never ends... you just don't want it to be as annoying as that song. With a warm embrace, the practice is to be present to your life and take care of the beautiful One that you are. This Easebook is a great way to begin that journey, not only for yourself but also for everyone else around you. Remember in Chapter 1 how you described what it would mean to have greater ease in your life? Come back to that now. Don't lose the feeling sense it evoked and the mindset of possibility it provided. When you're feeling satisfied, happy, and healthy, you're able to meet the demands of your life in a way that is regenerating and nourishing, not depleting. Things seem to fall into place as ease becomes a bigger part of your personal landscape.

Rest assured that this Easebook isn't asking that you drop your life and run away. Even though some days you may fantasize about that, you love the people and things in your life... that's why you've been supporting them for so long. They don't need to go away but you do deserve to let go of some of the chaos and overtaxing busyness. When you do, the important things will come to the surface and be more visible, making it easier to pay attention and attend to them on purpose. And the best part of this is you! There's so much to learn and reconnect with about yourself - it's truly exciting! So continue the wonderful and fun journey of discovering your ever-changing and ever-beautiful self. You're worth it!

5

LET THE JOURNEY BEGIN!

You cannot pour from an empty cup.
~ Unknown ~

There are two approaches in how to best use this Easebook. One is to take it with you wherever you go and refer to it throughout the day, making entries as your day proceeds. The other is to keep it safely nestled by your favorite reflection place or bed, making notations in the morning and evening. Do whatever works for you but, if you prefer morning and evening times, it can be helpful to come up with a system that will help you remember to engage with the activities throughout the day... strategically placed sticky-notes, calendar items, reminders or a habit app on your phone, or a copy of any of the pages. Don't rely on memory alone; your brain is already overloaded with everything else you have to remember. Developing a new skillset takes time and practice so set yourself up for greater success with reminders that work.

Also, if it's easier, instead of trying to integrate everything that is being offered, you can focus on one particular section for a week (Waking Up, Self-Care, Mindfulness, Body Care, Reflections). Stay committed to at least this one section, adding another one as the weeks go on. Being diligent with this one section will still influence the rest so don't worry that you're not doing enough. It's best to do a section well than to be haphazard and uncommitted.

Take a peak at the daily journals in the back of this Easebook now so you have an idea of what's being talked about as you walk through the different sections. You'll notice there are many different touch points and activities that directly and indirectly relate to the important Fabulous FRESH Five, the basic components that promote health, balance, and well-being.

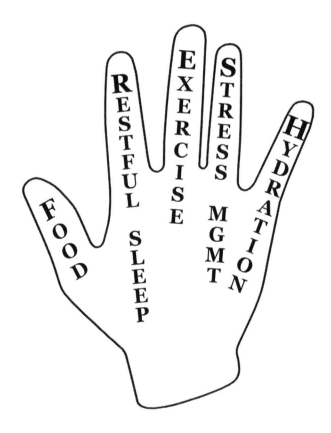

WAKING UP

Today I feel...

Take a few slumbering minutes before you jump out of bed in the morning or a few quiet moments as you enjoy that first cup of coffee or tea to check in and ask "How am I doing today?" Scan yourself. What does your body feel like - rested, tired, achy? What emotions are present - excitement, contentment, worry? Observing the mind, is it busy planning and preparing already, is there spaciousness, is it settled and calm? Overall, how do you feel? Offering attention to yourself and your inner world is one of the most precious gifts you can give yourself. Whatever you discover is the best information to be used when creating your day as this is your GPS starting point for everything else that lies ahead. When you know your inner landscape and location, you can direct yourself appropriately and stay in the driver's seat.

My Happiness Scale 1 -10

This is another GPS data point. Again, no self-recrimination, just information. Remember, mindfulness just wants to know what's real.

Decide for yourself what your 1-10 scale represents but it might be something like:

10 = Life is awesome. I'm awesome. Feeling like it's all working well.

5 = Ya, it's going good. I could use a bit more lift but I'm engaged.

1 = Feeling pretty low and down in the dumps. Up is my direction today.

Know that the Happiness Scale number doesn't define you but simply gives you a good idea of where you're at in this moment. If you're a 9, super. If you're a 5, OK. If you're a 2, good to know. Your Happiness Scale number can help shape what you put on your Self-Care list or what you decide will be your intention for the day.

If you liken the Happiness Scale to a weather report, it's easiest to plan your travel for the day when you have a better idea of the weather conditions. If it's raining, you can prepare for the rain by bringing an umbrella. If it's sunny, you may bring sunglasses or a hat to protect from overexposure. Whatever the weather condition, you make adjustments and prepare accordingly, even if you don't necessarily like the condition or it isn't what you hoped it to be.

So if you're 9 and sunny... awesome. Keep that sun shining and enjoy the warmth. If you're 3 and feeling stormy, protect yourself with some nourishing layers of self-care... a conversation with a friend, uplifting and positive self-talk, slowing the pace of the day, extra meditation or self-love breaks. Work with the conditions and elements that are present instead of getting frustrated by them. Also, remember that the weather is always changing so try to avoid getting fixated on its current condition. Flowing with what is seems to lighten things up without lots of effort.

I slept _____ hours

Without a doubt, sleep is one of the most essential components of a healthy body and mind; physically, mentally, emotionally, neurologically, relationally, spiritually, everythingly. Think for a moment... how well do you function without a good night sleep? Or perhaps sleeplessness has been such a big part of your life that it doesn't register how tired you really are. If you're like most go-go professionals in this sleep deprived society, you get an average of six or less hours of restful sleep every night, much less than the recommended 7.5 to 8.5 hours.

To put the necessity of good sleep into context, here are a few important facts about this Fabulous FRESH Five and its impact:

> Sleep is a precious time where working memory has a chance to get organized, giving the brain time to process and consolidate the information from all the day's activities. Besides being important for problem-solving and reasoning ability, working memory creates those

folders and filing cabinets that are filled will all sorts of information, the ones you pick through when you're trying to remember something. "What's the name of that person? Oh, I know... it's on the tip of my tongue." Without adequate sleep, not only are those filing cabinets half empty but the folders are all messed up and you can't find anything. Details are lost and the Game of Names is never won.

Inadequate sleep reduces your ability to stay alert and focused on a given task (bye-bye concentration), negatively impacts your decision-making process ("I have no idea what I should do!!"), weakens your long-term memory (it's not just an age thing after all), along with a decline in a whole range of other cognitive abilities ("I need my brain!").

Do you struggle with your weight and nasty cravings? Many hormones rebalance at night including ghrelin and leptin, two key contributors to appetite control and satiability levels. When these two are out of balance, you eat more and are less able to gauge when you're full... a poor combination for your waistline.

Have you ever noticed that you tend to eat more sweets, simple carbs, and crunchy food when you're tired? Or perhaps you have more coffee and caffeinated items than you'd really like. Unhealthy food becomes an easy choice as your body is looking for quick boosts of energy to get you through the day. Willpower and self-control require energy, going right out the window when sleep is low. You don't have the energy reserves to self-regulate, regroup, and convince yourself "not now". And, to continue the vicious cycle, all that caffeine and processed food interferes with being able to get a restful night sleep.

Are you sicker more often or have a harder time recovering from a basic cold or simple cut? If your immune system is taxed and doesn't have the resources to repair and recover, it's harder to stay healthy. Dis-ease begets disease. Ongoing sleep deficiency has been linked to an increased risk of heart disease, high blood pressure, diabetes, stroke, and kidney disease, just to name a few. It also makes chronic illnesses like fibromyalgia, arthritis, COPD, and asthma harder to manage.

Emotional regulation and stress management plummet when you're exhausted. Little things don't flow off your back and everything can feel prickly. Situations that normally wouldn't bother you now become the objects of disdain, frustration, and persistent rumination. It's easy to take comments and basic inquiry questions out of context, making interactions less productive and more destructive. Without energy reserves, you may get weepy at the slightest thing, snap without appropriate provocation, or completely shut down and isolate yourself. Any of this sound familiar?

~~~~~~~~~~~~~~~~~~~~~~~~~~~~~~~~~~~~

A few things that can support deeper sleep and more rest:

~~~~~~~~~~~~~~~~~~~~~~~~~~~~~~~~~~~~~

Sanctuary. When you walk into your bedroom, does it feel like a private cocoon that you could easily wrap yourself in or is it disheveled with laundry strewn about everywhere, piles of books or pillows blocking the bed, cluttered bureau tops, and dust bunnies hopping about? Is the air fresh and clean like the morning dew or is it stale and stagnated, as if a wet bath towel has been trying to dry in the corner for days?

It's hard to relax and get comfortable if your environment feels messy and cluttered. It's well worth any effort taken to create a space that's inviting and welcoming, one that honors the sacredness of the bedroom and rest. Soothing wall colors, comfy bedding, a few decorative plants, and string lights or candles all fit the bill. You can also add some lavender sprigs or scents which are energetically soothing and relaxing.

Bedtime. Setting boundaries around sleep is important. Just like your kids have a regular bedtime, have yours be non-negotiable and one that you can stick to even on the weekends. As a creature of habit, your body and brain will respond favorably to this consistency in routine so be diligent in creating personal boundaries here.

On average, 7.5 to 8.5 of restful sleep provides the most benefit. If you're coming up short, one thing you can do is start going to bed 15 minutes earlier every three to four days until you're at your desired number of hours. It's hard for the brain and body to adjust to massive shifts in sleep time (think about the trouble around daylight savings time, especially in the spring when you lose an hour) so these small incremental changes can make it easier to develop new bedtime habits.

Transition Routine. Develop a bedtime routine that will create ease and offer a peaceful and distinct transition from the day. Some positive pre-bed activities:

- ✓ Complete this Easebook's *TODAY'S REFLECTION* section
- ✓ Yoga or some gentle stretches
- ✓ Meditation (**http://bit.ly/EverydayEaseMeditations**), prayer, or sitting quietly to just Be
- ✓ Break away from technology at least an hour before bed
- ✓ Long bubble bath
- ✓ Make love, slowly and sensually
- ✓ Read to your kids
- ✓ Enjoy your partner with light conversation or laughter

- ✓ Take a slow walk around the neighborhood
- ✓ Read something that's light and interesting, avoiding material that's too thought-provoking or stimulating
- ✓ Crossword puzzle, sudoku, jigsaw puzzle, solitaire
- ✓ Knit, crochet, needlepoint
- ✓ Coloring book, sketch, paint
- ✓ Gaze at the moon and stars
- ✓ Fold laundry or a quick pick-up around the house
- ✓ Chamomile or a relaxing herbal tea
- ✓ Prep for tomorrow: clothes out, lunches made, business priorities listed, calendar reviewed
- ✓ Hanging out with your favorite 2- or 4-legged
- ✓ Add your own:

_____

_____

_____

Sounds. If you're a light sleeper or live in an area where there's lots of extraneous noise that disrupts your sleep, try using earplugs, easy-listening background music, or a white noise machine. If your partner snores, negotiate sleeping areas or get a medical consult for this issue. Snoring can be a sign of a serious health problem, made even worse when no one is getting good sleep.

Sights. Keep the room as dark as possible. Shut curtains, have room-darkening shades, wear an eye mask, turn the LED clock to face the wall, use side lamps in favor of bright overhead lighting, and remove any objects of light that might interfere with dimming the room.

Electronics. Pull those plugs at least an hour before bedtime… and keep them out of the bedroom so they don't ding, ping, or light up at night. Whatever your electronic gadget may be, flip the switch so that your brain can flip its switch with ease. Many electronic devices emit blue light which has been shown to interfere with the natural product of melatonin, a hormone that contributes to the body's internal circadian rhythm. Switch to reading a good book, coloring, journaling, connecting with your partner, or spending time with this Easebook.

Late Day Eating. Try to avoid eating anything a few hours before bedtime, giving your body a chance to digest any food you've recently eaten. It can be helpful to reduce the amount of food consumed at dinnertime (typically the biggest meal of the American day) and to avoid late-night snacking whenever possible (oftentimes driven by emotional hunger versus physical hunger). If you have lots of gas, bloating, burping, acid reflux, or other digestive issues, take a look at your food consumption - content, timing, quantity - and make adjustments. Eating smaller quantities of healthy, easily digestible food earlier in the evening can help offset many of these issues.

Incorporating mindful eating into your food experience, savoring the taste by eating slower, and chewing your food into small digestible pieces is a super way to support healthy consumption. It also helps in absorbing the nutrients more easily, has you feeling fuller faster, and has you eating less without a sense of deprivation. You'll play with mindful eating as part of this Easebook's Mindful Activities so take note how it impacts your sleep.

Check the Label. Know your medications. Check with your physician or pharmacist to see what effects your medications might have on your sleep, even over-the-counter ones. The last thing you want is to work on getting healthier in one area and depleting yourself in another.

Concerns. Please consult your medical professional for any specific questions or concerns you have regarding your particular sleep patterns and habits. There are many things that impact quality and quantity of sleep so you'll want to have any new changes, old detrimental habits, and anomalies checked with a sleep professional. Sleep is important enough to address any concerns.

~~~~~~~~~~~~~~~~~~~~~~~~~~~~~~~~~~

Getting back to the Easebook segments...

~~~~~~~~~~~~~~~~~~~~~~~~~~~~~~~~~~

I'm looking forward to...

What is something that excites you about today? What gives you a sense of joyful anticipation, inspiration, and a positive view of the hours to come? Is it a planned lunch with a good friend, visiting with someone you haven't seen in a while, going to zumba or kickboxing, blocked time to work on a big project, a calendar that's not stuffed to the gills, or some quiet time alone? Whatever it is that you're looking forward to, write it down and have it be a positive foundation for the day.

My intention for the day

Attention follows intention. Purposefully setting the tone for the day and how you're going to approach it can make all the difference between it being smooth and easy and it falling apart. Sure, stuff will happen but success is more likely when you set the stage for it with an intentional mindset. The subconscious will direct your attention to things that support your expected view so enjoy what you ask for and its inexplicable fruition.

Take a few moments in the morning to be present to yourself, smile, and actively decide how you want your day to be and the energy you want to offer yourself and others. From a perspective of self-care, what do your heart and inner guides say? By purposefully setting your intention for the day, you're basically calling in the Universe and saying "Hey, let's have THIS be what my day is about. Let's make it happen!" This powerful activity may be the lever that switches an OK day to a good day, a good day to a great day, and a great day to being even better than you could have imagined.

As a connector to the energy of creating your intention, you may like to begin the day with this gatha poem from Thich Nhat Hanh:

Waking up this morning I smile
knowing there are 24 brand new hours before me.
I vow to live fully in each moment
and look at all Beings with eyes of compassion.

SELF-CARE

Everything you do either fuels you or drains you and, while there's usually an ebb and flow for this, you want to do all you can to have your fuel gauge be full. Being on empty in the middle of Busy Street is not a happy place.

Along with setting your intention in planning the day, it's important to schedule and make room for those things that nourish and revitalize you. Waiting for the time to show up is a lost cause. How many times have you said "When blah blah blah happens, then I can take a break.", "When everything lines up perfectly, including the moon and the stars,...". Ya, put those never-gonna-happens out to pasture and make a conscious decision to take charge of your self-care.

As was mentioned earlier, if it's been a while since you've said YES to you, it might feel a bit challenging to all of a sudden do that. Break yourself in with a pace that works. That doesn't mean you have permission to delay putting yourself at the top of the list but there is this thing called the reality of life. At a minimum, integrate one self-care activity for the first week, increasing the number of activities as the weeks progress. In this way, habits of self-care form and become part of your daily routine.

After you're established, the request for *Self-Care* is to have three activities every day. They don't have to be huge, like taking a whole day off to trek a mountain or doing a full day of pampering with a deep tissue massage, reiki, pedicure, and a fancy lunch (although these are awesome choices). Little points of refueling through the day are perfect. As little as ten minutes of purposeful time and attention on yourself goes a long way. Plus, small self-care activities are easier to maintain so you're more likely to do them on a regular basis.

Here are 25 great ideas that will fuel your inner awesomeness:

1. Take a walk - local park, walking trail, around the neighborhood or business building
2. Meditation - guided or on your own. Even five minutes can make a huge difference, having you feel grounded, centered, and present. For the guided meditations that come with this Easebook, go to **http://bit.ly/EverydayEaseMeditations**.
3. Movement break in between meetings or activities
4. Take a break from technology: unplug for a an hour, half a day, or one whole day every week
5. Swing on a swing and feel like a kid again
6. Sit in the sun and absorb the beautiful rays and Vitamin D

7. Laugh - funny video, jokes, tickle fights with the kids, laughter yoga, being silly, hanging out with a comical colleague
8. Essential oils - lavender is great for calming and soothing the senses
9. Make a super delicious and nutritious meal with a new food
10. Body scrub in the shower
11. Wash your face clean of all make-up and notice how beautiful you are just as you are
12. Dance - the kitchen is a great spot if you don't have a formal class or local dancehall
13. Play with a pet
14. Take a breath break and connect to this vital element
15. Open and shift your energy systems with hula hooping
16. Lay or walk on the warm Earth to feel supported and grounded, capturing those negative ions that will rebalance your energy state
17. Enjoy a quiet cup of tea
18. Talk to a favorite non-fix-me friend who knows how to listen
19. Floss your teeth - your dentist will love you, too
20. Get dirty in the garden, play with plants, arrange flowers
21. Sit quietly to look at the sky, birds, clouds, and trees. Do you see yourself in the cloud?
22. Read an inspiring or spiritual book
23. Use the brain in a different way with a jigsaw puzzle
24. Take a delicious nap
25. Listen to music that's befitting your mood - from pulsing dance to calming classic

Some things that take a bit more time and planning, but still yummy for your soul:

1. Lunch with a friend or your partner

2. Massage, bodywork, reiki, or an energy session

3. A favorite hobby like painting, drawing, sketching, scrapbooking, woodworking, photography, needle point, birding

4. Manicure / pedicure

5. Awesome sex

6. Visiting the ocean, lake, river, or other natural water source

7. Yoga, pilates, Zumba, tai chi, or any other class you enjoy

8. Listening to a book on tape during your commute

9. A longer hike or venture into nature

10. Picnic at the park

Since you know yourself better, list some additional options that are fun for you:

1. _____

2. _____

3. _____

4. _____

5. _____

6. _____

7. _____

8. _____

Today's Mindful Activity

So much of your day is routined. This doesn't mean that it's all bad but it does mean that the lack of freshness makes it easy to drift into inattentiveness and complacency. The human brain habituates to similar situations and adapts pretty quickly to sameness. Just think of the excitement you have for a new hairstyle or car. How long before it fades into "the regular" and no longer gets noticed?

The mind tends to always be searching for something engaging to "chew on". If daily activities become wallpaper, the bored mind may keep itself stimulated with mental and/or physical multitasking. When you're multitasking, while it can feel like you're being productive and industrious darting from one thing to another, this switching back and forth actually has the brain and body feeling unsettled, anxious, and out of flow. Instead of being connected to what you're doing and who you're with, there's a separation from the actual experience since you're not spending much time or attention there. How much of what's in front of you are you missing?

Also, when the mind has free reign to go where it wants, it usually wanders into the dreadful past or drums up things to be worried about in the future. Unfortunately, unless you're fresh in a new love relationship, your mind doesn't wander to highlighting everything that's right with your life or all the ways you've been blessed. Negativity bias, part of a basic survival alert system that warns you of danger, can be a pretty tough contender when left to its own devices. Thoughts create reality so, if you're constantly seeking and searching what's wrong, this has a huge impact on your health and wellness. Over time, without periods of consistent coming back and reflection to what's real and true, anxiety and stress can accumulate and deplete your vital resources, eventually leading to depression and burnout.

To create a truer connection with yourself and your moments, you'll be engaging with mindful activities over the course of these six weeks. You'll be tapping into the benefits of mindfulness that were talked about in Chapter 2 by having specific daily activities as your training ground. These activities are things that you're already doing but probably not paying much attention to, meaning your mind may be unconsciously dwelling on ugly things and ruminating far away from truth. And while the mindful activities you'll be playing with are fairly simple and easy, it's not the level of difficulty of the activity that's the focus. The main focus will be on staying present to yourself as you're engaged in the activity... with an unintended, but often amusing or enlightening, gift of becoming aware of how *not* present you are. By focusing on what you're actually doing, the mind has less opportunity to wander aimlessly in a thousand different directions, thus easing the stress and tension that accumulates when you're not paying attention and specifically engaged.

Play along. Be yourself. Have fun.

Being mindful takes practice and, the more you do it, the more natural and integrated it becomes. Over the six weeks of this Easebook, six mindful activities will be offered, a new one every week. This means that you'll have seven days to practice with each activity, sufficient time to get familiar, explore, and experiment. And don't worry... since the mindful activities are things you're already doing every day, there's no need to shuffle your schedule around to accommodate them.

As you engage with the activity, be as present and tuned in as you can, with a sense of curiosity and beginner's mind, as if you were doing it for the first time. Questions that invoke inquiry:

* *What's here that I haven't noticed before?*
* *How is my body experiencing this activity?*
* *Where's my mind? Am I here?*
* *How strong is the urge to do something else instead of staying right here?*
* *How does it feel when I'm here and focused on the activity?*

Sometimes remembering to do the activity is the biggest challenge so create a reminder system that works for you. You might put a sticky note with a smiley face or a big letter "M" by where the activity takes place as a visual reminder.

~~~~~~~~~~~~~~~~~~~~~~~~~~~~~~~~~~~~

The six mindful activities you'll be playing with:

~~~~~~~~~~~~~~~~~~~~~~~~~~~~~~~~~~~~

Brushing Teeth

You've been brushing your teeth at least twice a day since you were a little bitty youngster. It's such a routined activity that you may barely notice you're doing it unless you've got toothpaste dripping down your chin or you have gum pain or a toothache.

When you brush your teeth as a Mindful Activity, spend time noticing what you're *actually* doing during that time; getting dressed, reading, talking on the phone, putting on make-up, running after the kids, thinking about work and mentally preparing for the day... the list is endless.

The request is to come back to the brushing of the teeth. That's it. Be present and notice the routine you've established for brushing around the mouth, the contact of the brush to your gums, the sensation of the paste in your mouth, the spitting, rinsing, how your mouth feels afterwards... the whole thing. Teeth brushing is a time of important physical self-care and, by being present, you can establish it as a time of important mental self-care as well.

Washing Hands

Just like brushing your teeth, washing hands can be an autopilot activity with the mind having free-range to go in many different and discursive directions. As a Mindful Activity, when you wash your hands, notice everything there is to the washing; turning on the water, the temperature of the water, wetting the hands, lathering with soap, rubbing the hands together to clean, rinsing, and drying off. As you wash your hands in this way, you'll wash your mind of busyness and clean your moment.

Mindful Eating

Mindless eating is something that even the most tuned in person does. With so many things pulling for your attention, it's easy to get distracted instead of paying attention to eating and the food that's in front of you. You may eat while working at your desk, driving from here to there, bored in front of the TV, or talking with someone. How many times have you looked down at your bowl or plate, surprised to see it all gone but not remembering the eating? Mindless eating has you consuming in a way that adds additional calories and food selections that might not match your preferences or desires. Also, as food can be a poor substitution for healthy emotional support, there's even more reason to be aware of what's happening when you eat. Food can be used to soothe the full range emotions from loneliness, depression, anger, frustration, and boredom. Overall, mindless eating has the capacity to negatively impact physical and mental health so it's definitely one to watch.

For the week of mindful eating, completely tune in to eating the first five minutes of a designated meal or snack, one that you'll have more freedom for quiet and concentration. Turn your attention away from screens, conversations, driving, reading, or any other non-eating activity and become present to the delicious and nutritious food that's in front of you. Notice the shapes, colors, textures, and scents of the food. Notice the actions of chewing, breaking the food into small digestible pieces, the changes in texture and taste, swallowing, and receiving the nutrients. Place the fork or spoon down in between bites, creating a gap between mouthfuls and getting away from the "shoveling" effect. With mindful eating, you'll add a lot more than physical nutrition. This activity can be quite enlightening... and yummy. Enjoy!

Walk With Presence

For this Mindful Activity, choose a hallway, walkway, or set of stairs that you frequent throughout the day. Every time you walk this area, be attentive to your breath, body, and mind. Feel the breath as it supports each step, noticing that each step is supported by the floor underneath. Notice your feet and the action of moving your body, how the hips pivot, and how the legs pick themselves up without instruction. Instead of letting your mind get busy reviewing what you just left or planning what's ahead, pull it back and let it rest on the movements of your body, your breath, and the walking. Although it's beneficial to slow your walking pace down a bit since the mind rushes when the body rushes, you can walk at your regular pace. The important part is your attentive connection to the walking, not the speed of the walking. When you arrive at your destination with this type of embodied presence, you're guaranteed to arrive fresher and with greater awareness of what's there.

Stop Signs And Stop Lights

Putt, putt, putt. You're driving along doing errands, hauling the kids around, commuting to and from work. As you come to an intersection, while the car's motion is halted because of a stop sign or stop light, it doesn't stop you. You keep right on going in your head, busy thinking about this, that, and the other thing. As your mind time-travels in and out of the past and future within the happy-sad-mad trio, it's easy to lose track of where you really are. Have you ever had the experience of driving for miles and miles without noticing any of it, amazed that you got to your destination safely? Thank you internal autopilot! But that autopilot can also have you arriving at your destination with lots of unnecessary and unintended baggage, bringing your worries along for the ride and having you feeling quite disheveled.

With stop signs and stop lights as your Mindful Activity, use the stop signage you encounter to do just that - STOP. Stop and check in with your body: how is your posture, is your body tilting to one side or the other, how are your hands on the steering wheel, where is the breath in the body? Stop and check in with the mind: what stream of thoughts are running in the foreground and the background? As you STOP, bring your mind's attention completely back to the present moment. Keep your attention on driving and being in the car as long as you can, "waking up" whenever you encounter another stop sign or stop light. Practicing presence when you drive supports your presence during other off-road travels through the day.

Showering

How many people do you shower with every day? No, not literally, silly. Figuratively. It's quite common to share your shower with your partner, colleagues, last night's news story, your child's teacher, work projects, the neighbor's dog that won't stop barking, your dental hygienist, and even random grocery clerks. As the mind drifts in and out of planning for the day or recollecting past moments, the shower stall can fill up with many other bodies.

When you shower, shower yourself with your full attention. Tune in to your amazingly magnificent body, the one beautiful vessel you've been gifted with that's all yours and no one else's. As you shower and wash your body, bring appreciation and gratitude to each body part for the specific function it performs and how it's always working to keep you healthy and strong. Notice the uniqueness of your body, how one arm is different than the other, the softness or roughness of your skin, the shape of the ankle and toes. Even if you don't particularly like all of its parts, this beautiful body is yours. Loving and caring for it is offering yourself love and care. Mindful showering can transform the entire relationship you have with your body. When you love yourself completely, everything seems easier.

Choose Your Own

A space is available in the daily Easebook pages for you to add your own Mindful Activity, either as a replacement of the suggested one or as an addition to. From the examples above, you've got the idea of what to do - be present and tune in. By focusing *right here*, you'll avoid being *over there... and there.*

Other things you might like to choose to be fully present to:

- ✓ Putting on your socks or pants
- ✓ Buttoning a shirt or blouse
- ✓ Putting on make-up
- ✓ Brushing your hair
- ✓ Feeding a pet
- ✓ Opening doors
- ✓ Sipping a cup of tea or coffee
- ✓ Washing a dish
- ✓ Making the bed
- ✓ Folding laundry
- ✓ Going to the bathroom
- ✓ Watering plants
- ✓ Cleaning your eye or sun glasses
- ✓ A part of your work-out routine
- ✓ Removing shoes or coat
- ✓ Chopping vegetables
- ✓ Listening to or singing a song
- ✓ Organizing your desk
- ✓ Answering the phone and speaking to the other person
- ✓ Writing a priority or a to-do list
- ✓ Leaving the office for the day

There are a million ways you can be mindful through the day. Pick one and try it on for a week. It's one small step to being more present to your life. And don't forget to have a reminder system for your Mindful Activity so you keep engaged through the day: a sticky note by where the activity takes place, a reminder or habit app on your phone, a conscious dedication to connect the activity with mindful presence.

PEACFUL PAUSES

Peacefully pausing periodically through the day, for even just ten seconds, can make all the difference between a day realized and a day disheveled. Pausing helps slow down the speed of your busy go-go train, offering a momentary resting place so you can refuel your energy and recognize where you really are. If you're out of gas, you can refuel with some stretches, water, or healthy food. If you've unknowingly been carrying someone else's luggage or a heavy burden, you can put it down. If you're agitated or frustrated, you can take care of that in a skillful way. If you're feeling fantastic, you can recognize, rejoice, and enjoy it. Pausing with a moment of mindfulness is a beautiful grounding point from which to take the next best step. Without this pausing, the train keeps going a thousand miles an hour and, sooner or later, it's going to crash.

So what do you do when you Peacefully Pause? Stop, check in, and see what's going on for you in your body, mind, and whole being. Noticing the breath is a fantastic first step, gently guiding you back to your body for a quick reset. Place a hand on the heart and/or belly to deepen this breath-body connection. As your attention to the breath increases, the body will naturally calm with the mind slowly following. To increase the presence and peace from this pause, take ten slow breaths, dropping the shoulders and letting your whole body settle as you breath out. As you glide into this relaxation response, continue to keep your attention on the breath and the body breathing, letting yourself soften, relax, release, and settle. Feel free to pause for ten seconds or ten minutes, whatever fits the moment and the time you have available.

When do you Peacefully Pause? You can do it anytime throughout the day but, to begin making it a regular practice, it's helpful to create an association with another activity. Attaching a Peaceful Pause to transition times, when you move from one activity to another, is perfect. For example, every time you get in your car you can take a moment to peacefully pause before you start the engine. Make an agreement with yourself that this is what you'll do at the time (with a sticky note as a reminder in the beginning). By attaching a Peaceful Pause to this sort of regular activity, you'll be incorporating pauses throughout the day and creating a healthy peace habit in no time.

Some suggestions for when to Peacefully Pause:

✓ Coming back to your desk
✓ Before you eat a meal
✓ Waiting for a computer program or system to load
✓ Before standing up after you've put your shoes on
✓ Before you turn the car engine on or after you've shut it off
✓ Waiting for a meeting to begin
✓ The space in between tasks: the transition
✓ After washing your hands
✓ Waiting for water to boil
✓ Standing in line

Decide ahead of time when you'll be pausing so it's not haphazard and left to pure recollection. Also, work with only one Peaceful Pause per week. This will help establish a more consistent practice of integrating mindfulness into your day. After a week, keep pausing with that one activity and add another Peaceful Pause activity. Over time, your level of present moment awareness will be much greater and you'll have a whole new set of eyes on old experiences.

Note that, even though there are ten Peaceful Pause paw prints listed in the Easebook for each day, this doesn't mean that you need the activity to happen ten times every day. They are simply there to give you many opportunities.

BODY CARE

Hydration

Hydration, a component of the Fabulous FRESH Five, is essential to brain and body health. Besides the breath, water is one of the most necessary ingredients for survival. Every cell, organ, and tissue needs water to function properly. Water regulates your body temperature, helps detoxify and keep your body clean of impurities and waste products, lubricates joints, keeps your skin from drying, and transports nutrients so you have energy to do the things you want to do. If you're dehydrated, your cells can't pass information from one to the other and normal tasks are more challenging. You might experience brain fog, have a harder time focusing, have memory issues, and be less emotionally regulated. Chronic dehydration may lead to constipation, kidney stones, cholesterol problems, as well as muscle and joint damage. Oh, what a little water can do!

Dehydration is like how a kitchen sponge is in the morning... dry, hard, and practically impenetrable. If you were to try and clean up a spill on the counter with the sponge like that, you wouldn't be able to do it. The sponge needs to be wet before it can absorb any other material. It only works well when it's hydrated, just like you.

To start your day off right, enjoy a nice glass of tepid or warm water. Yes, this is even before that highly anticipated first cup of coffee. Unless you're a magician, you're not drinking when you're sleeping and thus you wake up in a drought situation, just like that dry kitchen sponge. And, for an added boost, add some lemon to the water. It tastes great and your body will love the increased alkalinity, important in maintaining health and reducing inflammation and disease.

Stay hydrated throughout the day by having clean water readily available. Choose glass, metal, or BPA-free water containers, skipping the plastics. There are chemicals in the plastic (including endocrine disruptors) that can leach into the water from the plastic bottle... and then into your body. Gross! Also, in support of Mother Earth, please use these safe reusable containers. The manufacturing process of plastics is extremely harsh and it can take the volume of three plastic bottles full of water to make one plastic bottle. Talk about a waste! Even if you recycle, there's a significant environmental cost to that as well; the oceans and lands are filled with plastic. Given all of this, along with the shortage of clean water in this world, it's easy to support greater individual and global health. A glass, metal, or BPA-free water bottle costs roughly $10-20, a pretty cheap investment that offers compounding returns. Simply put, hydrate with clean water in a clean way.

Veggies

 To represent all of the main food groups in the Fabulous FRESH Five, only vegetables are tracked in the Easebook. Why? Plain and simple: Typically the number of vegetables eaten on a daily basis represents overall nutritional intake. If you're eating lots of vegetables, you're more likely to be eating the right amount of healthy protein, grains, fats, and fruit.

Vegetables are a major source of vitamins and minerals, providing natural energy for your cells. Most vegetables are low in calories, are fiber-rich, and have no cholesterol. There are hundreds of vegetables to choose from, each containing unique nutritional components that are essential to health. A colorful plate is a healthy plate.

Vegetables can be added to everything from omelettes to soups, sandwiches to side dishes, and casseroles to main meals. They can be sautéed, souped, roasted, baked, mashed, fried, spiraled, raw, fermented, juiced, and in smoothies. And many are super convenient, already packaged in their own little container so they're handy dandy to take wherever you go.

Before you buy vegetables, grab a hold of the **Dirty Dozen** and **Clean 15** lists. These lists refer to the top vegetables and fruit that, respectively, are the most and least pesticide contaminated. The lists, generated by EWG (Environmental Working Group www.ewg.org), changes slightly every year so a simple internet search will provide the most up to date version.

The condition of our commercial agricultural system is such that there are more and more pesticides and chemicals being used in all stages of food production: seed generation, crop growth and maintenance, harvesting, storage. Soils are being depleted of their natural energies and crop seeds are being manufactured in the science lab with GMO / GE (genetically modified organisms / genetically engineered) ingredients. In an attempt to expand and streamline standard food sources, the agriculture conglomerates have gone haywire and moved furthest away from Mother Nature. The current agricultural system is unhealthy and unsustainable - for yourself, your family, and the Earth. There's much more to this vital topic; some great first-hit resources are Institute for Responsible Technology (www.responsibletechnology.org) and Environmental Working Group (www.ewg.org).

Needless to say, organic and GMO-free foods are your healthiest options. If budget is an obstacle to buying organic, you can feel safer eating commercially produced Clean 15 items. For the Dirty Dozen, however, you'll want to choose organic or at least GMO-free for these food items. The items on the Dirty Dozen list contain a high level of pesticides and contaminants which are not removed by simply washing the item.

You can also have lots of fun and grow your own veggies from organic seeds in pesticide-free soil. Start small and with easy-to-grow items like beans, radish, kale, lettuce, peas, summer squash, and cucumbers. You don't need a lot of space and planter pots can look great and do the trick (super for apartment and city dwellers). Growing your own food, even herbs, is a lot of fun for the whole family so get them involved and teach them about taking care of their health and well-being. These are lessons that will last a lifetime... plus getting your hands in the dirt is just plain good.

Some easy way to incorporate more veggies:

- ✓ Add one new veggie per week. There are lots of free recipes on the internet so have fun and experiment.

- ✓ Take a cooking class or follow along on-line cooking demonstrations.
- ✓ Keep your interest peaked by changing how you prepare veggies. You'll appreciate the different textures and flavors that come alive when you roast them in the oven, make a soup, create a 10-veggie salad, fine dice, mash, or spiral as a substitute for pasta noodles.
- ✓ Make your own veggie chips by cutting root veggies into thin slices, lightly coat with olive oil, add a little sea salt, and roast in the oven until crisp. Kale leaves are also great like this.
- ✓ Have a potluck vegetarian party and have folks bring recipe cards. It's a great way to try lots of new food without investing lots of time, energy, or money. Plus, it's a super fun way to hang out with friends.

There are eight veggie icons listed in the daily Easebook pages, each representing one adult serving (typically 1/2 - 1 cup depending upon the food). Standard daily intake recommendations are between five to twelve servings. Start where you are and do your best. Here's to your health!

My-Body-Thanks-Me Foods

In this section, celebrate how you've nourished yourself and helped your body to feel ggrreeeaatt. Perhaps you had a veggie omelette for breakfast, a salad with eight different ingredients including some lean protein and seeds, a protein smoothie on the way to the gym, a yummy soup or stew for dinner, or a crisp apple with cinnamon for a snack. Whatever you ate that had your body knowing you love and care for it, make note of it here. And if you had an off day with not-so-great foods or lots of take-out, don't beat yourself up. Figure out how that sort of eating day came together and begin again tomorrow - it's another day and another opportunity. Take a few moments now to plan your healthy foods for then.

Exercise and Movement

A moving body is a happy body. With so many hours spent sitting and staring at the computer, your beautiful vessel gets tight, constricted, and zapped of energy. Instead of reaching for caffeine or candy, regular movement throughout the day can have the brain and body working at its best without the negative effects from these artificial energy enhancers. In this electronic-driven society, sitting is the new health enemy, leading many people to a state of decline and aging far beyond their biological age would dictate.

For some people, the word "exercise" brings up images of drudgery, a reminder of times gone past where they struggled sticking with an exercise routine and spent more time fighting off shame and guilt thoughts than they did actually moving their body. None of those associations belong here and, if these images are true for you, begin to think of the word "movement" instead of "exercise". Movement is fun, spontaneous, freeing, flowing, exciting, and inviting to your body. With this simple switch in wording, you're more likely to enjoy whatever exercise you decide to do and are more likely to incorporate the activity into your daily routine.

With so much information available to the general public on exercise and movement (standard recommended amounts, precautions, physician clearance, etc.), just a brief description of the three main types of exercise are below. Here's to balancing life with another Fabulous FRESH Five!!

Cardiovascular

 Cardio is the best way to get the heart and blood pumping, condition the lungs, burn excess calories, improve muscle tone, and increase endurance. It's a fantastic way to reduce stress and the body's stress hormones, such as adrenaline and cortisol, while at the same time super for increasing the production of endorphins, your brain's feel-good neurotransmitters that are also the body's natural painkillers and mood elevators.

Suggestions: dance (perfect in the kitchen), hula-hoop, Zumba, speed walk, run, jog, swim, kickball, kickboxing, soccer, tennis, biking, rowing, jump rope, jumping jacks, ski, snowshoe, hiking, swimming, walking your pet, really great sex.

Strength Training

Want to feel strong and confident in both body and mind? Strength training can do that. Muscles deteriorate over time when they're not being consistently challenged so a regular program of strength training is a key component of lasting health. Strength training can also increase bone density and reduce the risk of osteoporosis, improve blood flow, build a stronger heart, and reduce your resting blood pressure. It helps control blood sugar, improves cholesterol levels, and improves your balance and coordination. Also (and you'll love this), strength training can help you manage or lose weight by increasing your resting metabolism. Muscle burns more energy than fat so you'll use up more calories, even if not much else about your routine has changed. Pretty sweet, right?

Suggestions: free weights at home or the gym, resistance machines (usually at the gym), resistance elastic bands (easy to take anywhere, great if you travel), a gallon of water as a weight, your body weight (great for wall push-ups), boot camp, kettle bells, stability ball, medicine ball, rock climbing.

Flexibility

Keeping muscles tone and ligaments pliable is important as you get older and want to keep the body strong, fit, and lean. Flexibility training also helps to improve balance, important as the body gets older and is more prone to falls and the associated long-lasting injuries. You certainly don't bounce like you used to.

For the workplace, stretching is pretty easy to incorporate and will have you feeling more alive, energized, and invigorated throughout the day.

- ✓ Take a 2 minute stretch break every hour.
- ✓ Incorporate leg lunges to open up hip-flexors and the front of the body which gets very tight from sitting all day and impacts the structural integrity of the body.
- ✓ Stretch your arms up, arcing over to open up the sides of the body.
- ✓ Swing the arms around like a spinner, letting them flop lazily, loosening torso tension and creating space in the spine.
- ✓ With one to two other people, have standing or walking meetings. They tend to be shorter, more productive, and more creative as everyone's thinking on their feet.
- ✓ Stretch anytime you're waiting… in line, for a meeting to start, water to boil, food to re-heat, computer program to load, etc.
- ✓ During conference calls or webinars, do some squats, lunges, and stretches as you listen with a headset.
- ✓ Before you plop yourself down coming back to your desk, take another 30 seconds to stretch. Make this a consistent practice.

Additional Suggestions: yoga, pilates, Barre, ballet, bosu ball, basic mindful stretching.

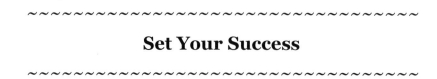

Set Your Success

Being prepared and ready for action is an earmark of success so list some exercise and movement activities you enjoy here so they'll be right at your fingertips when you start planning your activity time. Note the key word "enjoy". If you don't like doing it, you're not going to do it and pushing yourself to do something you don't really like or want to do oftentimes just feeds nasty guilt or a sense of shame. Let's avoid that! Don't give up on yourself too easily, though. Get out of your comfort zone and try something new. See these exercise and movement activities as wonderful ways to connect with your awesome self and body, helping your beautiful vessel stay strong and vibrant. Sometimes it's all in the attitude so tune in to how much you care and value yourself and your health. Let self-love be the warm-up.

For ideas on what to list below, look at the *Suggestions* above but also think outside the box for possibilities. Have nature be your playground, get a movement buddy, join a community class, do it as a family, participate in an on-site offering at work, check out YouTube and on-line videos, or hire a personal coach. There are lots of options.

Cardio   Strength   Flexibility

_____   _____   _____

_____   _____   _____

_____   _____   _____

_____   _____   _____

~~~~~~~~~~~~~~~~~~~~~~~~~~~~~~~~~~~~

Some Healthy Reminders:

✓ Even if you haven't exercised in years, don't worry. It's fantastic that you're taking action now in loving yourself more. Start where you are, without guilt, shame, or judgment.

✓ Get a physical exam if it's been a while or you have any medical concerns, especially if you haven't exercised in more than a year.

✓ Have a goal of at least thirty minutes every day, mixing up the three exercise-movement types throughout the week. For the days where a single timeframe of thirty minutes isn't possible, break that into three ten-minute segments. It'll quickly add up to your thirty minute commitment and makes it pretty doable. Excuses be gone!

✓ Put your exercise-movement time on your calendar so that it's part of your daily routine. Decide ahead of time to keep your commitment, feeling excited for this quality and energizing time with yourself.

✓ Keep a variety of exercise-movement activities going so you don't get bored but also notice the go-to ones that are a sure win. Keep these in your back pocket.

✓ Wear comfortable clothes during the day so you can move freely, even if you're sitting at your desk. Tight waistbands, bras, and shoes can cut off circulation and create physical tension. Comfort and fashion *can* go hand in hand.

~~~~~~~~~~~~~~~~~~~~~~~~~~~~~~~~~

Today's Appreciation For My Body

If you were to whisper sweet-nothings to your body, what would you say? What's the most heart-felt appreciation you could give?

Much of the time the body gets missed in the busyness of the day... unless it's not feeling well, gets injured, or isn't cooperating with the amount of strength or coordination needed. You may have a negative body image - for the whole thing or just parts: thighs, legs, arms, bust, butt, hair, etc. You may be angry with your body for a specific condition or chronic illness or be upset that it's holding onto weight that just won't release. Whatever your relationship with your body, this is a wonderful place in

78

to offer it whole-hearted appreciation every day. With appreciation comes gratitude, kindness, acceptance, and love. Love is the energy of transformation.

Some reflective questions:

* How does your body make you happy?
* How did it show up well and support your activities today? Perhaps you were tired with lackluster energy but your body kept going and made it possible to get done what needed to be done.
* What specific area might you be proud of or care deeply for?
* If there's a specific body part that causes you trouble, how can you offer it encouragement, appreciation, care, and gratitude?
* Imagine what life would be like without this part. What sense of appreciation and gratitude does *that* offer?

Here are some appreciation mantras you might like to share with yourself through the day. Pick one and take it with you. Write it on an index card, create an electronic background image for your phone or computer, put it in your lunchbox as a Love Note, or post some pictures or graphics that represent the feeling sense they evoke.

* *Thank you for carrying me around all day, dear body. I know I've been busy thinking of other things but I want to thank you deeply for all the support and energy you continue to give me. It makes everything possible.*
* *I love and accept my body just the way it is. This is my temple and makes loving life possible.*
* *It's okay to love myself now as I continue to evolve.*
* *Simply put, I am beautiful.*
* *My body is perfect and capable just the way it is.*

* *I am healthy, fit, and strong.*

* *I am so grateful for all that my body is still able to do for me. May grace and ease be mine.*

* *I am healthy and strong. I have plenty of energy to do everything I am called to do today.*

TODAY'S REFLECTION

Somewhere in your home, create a little quiet zone, a space and place that's just for you - away from the kids, your partner, the pets, and any household or work items. It could be a corner in your bedroom, a hide-away space on the porch overlooking the backyard, or an easy chair that wraps you in its cozy arms. Decorate this area with things that make you smile, colors that are soothing, and objects that draw you inward like candles or incense. Have a comfortable seating area with pillows and shams, ambiance lighting, and a few plants that bring nature indoors. This is a place where you feel nourished simply by being there.

As you finish your day, take some time to pause and check in, reflecting on the following questions. They'll help keep the day's events in a positive light and also set the tone for a nourishing and restful sleep.

What did I do well today?

Note the positive things you did, how you showed up, the energy, focus, and dedication you offered whatever was in front of you, how you managed to make lemonade out of lemons, and how you stuck with your commitments of better health and greater ease. How did you create the best day possible today? Positive reflection and self-talk focuses on the good and dismantles the inner critic so bring this recognition of what's working well into your psyche, esteem, confidence, and care bucket. Give yourself lots of praise and authentic acknowledgement. You deserve it! Don't forget... you're awesome! You're amazing! You're beautiful! You've done it... and you're doing it!

What did I learn from a challenging moment?

While you're moving forward in creating more ease, not every day will be easy. There'll be bumps, bruises, irritations, triggers, disagreements, relentless habits, and glorious dissatisfactions... all fodder for growth and development. As the saying goes, if you're not growing, you're dying.

Sometimes a challenge may be as simple as frustration rising when someone in front of you drives five miles under the speed limit for your entire commute. Sometimes it might be a nagging thought or worry you can't shake off that ruins your concentration and has you feeling nervous and tense. Sometimes it might be a disagreement with a co-worker or partner that reverberates through the rest of the day.

Whatever your challenge is, the mindful work is to recognize, understand, come to terms, and let it go as soon as possible. To help you do this, open your hand in the mindful position, placing the recollection of your challenging moment onto the palm. Take a few slow deep breaths to tune in to yourself, get centered and grounded, and then mentally step back to gain some perspective of the situation. From this witnessing view and without judgment or blame, reflect on these questions:

* *How did the difficulty come about? What led up to it happening?*
* *How did this situation impact my body? How did it drain my energy and activate stress hormones? What did it do to my breath and the level of tension in my body?*
* *Did my mind gear up for a fight and go into a defensive position or did I get fearful and want to avoid it all together or run away? How did that impact the situation?*

* *What old habits may have been activated by the situation? What parts were familiar?*
* *What would I have liked to have happened instead?*
* *What did I do well? How did I engage with new and better insights?*
* *What nuggets of personal growth and development can I take away from this situation?*

These reflections are done with a mindset of curiosity, care, kindness, self-respect, self-compassion, and love. You're not reflecting in order to ruminate, criticize, devalue or belittle, justify causes and conditions, or make anyone wrong... including yourself. It's simply to gain better awareness and understanding and to support your personal growth. By taking notice, adding a good attitude, and initiating positive action, you continue to get better and better.

There are millions of small growth moments in your life. Instead of shying away or masking them with busyness, take full advantage of becoming more finely tuned-in and aware of the complex and intricate Being you are. With awareness, understanding, and presence, you get to decide more about your life as new moments arise, building the all-important muscles of self-efficacy and resilience. No blame, shame, guilt, criticism, or reprimanding. Just care, attention, positive intent, personal trust, authenticity, and the realization that you're a human Being being human. And while you're totally super, you're not a super hero who does everything perfectly. Learn and grow. Grow and learn. This is the beauty of life.

Three words to celebrate me today:

It's really important to celebrate yourself and your successes every day, to give the same gratitude and appreciation that you give to others. Celebration keeps your strengths and goodness at the forefront, encouraging and motivating you to continue creating your best life. Without celebration, things just seem a bit tougher and less forgiving than they need to be.

As you wrap up your day, come up with three words that will have you feeling inspired, empowered, energized, and gloriously appreciative of who you are and how you showed up in your world. How would you describe yourself today? What were the delicious highlights? And if it was really challenging day, what strengths did you bring forth in meeting those challenges? These three words can serve as powerful mantras for the restful sleep ahead and set the tone for the beautiful day of tomorrow. Some possibilities:

confident	inspired	bold
passionate	fun	upbeat
steadfast	peaceful	self-assured
curious	resilient	warm
loving	go-getter	kind
daring	transparent	proficient
compassionate	diligent	skillful
fearless	empowered	efficient
balanced	strong	spirited
capable	vigorous	competent
courageous	clever	take-charge
playful	heart-filled	savvy
champion	tenacious	creative
hopeful	joyful	connected
graceful	energetic	effortless

Play along. Be yourself. Have fun.

6

EXPLORING THE EASEBOOK: SIX WEEKS OF YOU

The more you praise and celebrate life,
the more there is in life to celebrate.

~ Oprah Winfrey ~

Thank you, thank you, thank you for your amazing spirit and dedication. I have so much appreciation and gratitude to you for being here, for showing up for yourself, for putting down the mindset that keeps you last on your list, and for deciding that you are worth all the time and energy you need in order to have your life feeling more fulfilled and satisfied. YES! The next six weeks will be a really exciting time as you give yourself the space and freedom to grow, refine, and define yourself even more. Embrace it all.

As you offer yourself kindness and compassion with the Easebook, life will feel like it's coming together. Things that felt irritating before will begin to have much less effect and random smiles will appear on your face. You'll begin to make choices that are discerning and connected to your intuition and true desires without a big discussion. You'll know what to do without second guessing yourself, feeling confident and satisfied even if the situation changes. You'll be mastering your life instead of having it master you.

This energy of self-care and love will spread to everyone you meet, even if it's in the electronic ethers. As ease permeates your views, thoughts, speech, and actions, you'll attract this in the people you meet and the experiences you have. Those around you will feel heard, seen, and supported by your presence. Then these wonderful people will go out into their world with that energy, adding this presence and positivity to the relationships they have with others. Like dominos tumbling, the world is becoming a better place... because you're taking care to love yourself strong. You never knew you could be the cause of so much good, did you? This is how big change happens - the small steps of the individual compound and multiply to effect the collective. And with a progressive feedback loop, everything you do in kindness and care comes back to you with more energy and vitality. You started it... a continuation of peace and ease throughout your world, all by taking care of you! Thank you, thank you, thank you.

With lots of Peace and Love,
Shanti

Life isn't about finding yourself.
Life is about creating yourself.

~ George Bernard Shaw

WAKING UP   DAY 1   Date _____

Today I feel:

_____

My Happiness Scale 1 - 10 _____   I slept _____ hours

I'm looking forward to:

_____

My intention for the day:

_____

SELF-CARE   3 ways I'm going to care for myself:

1) _____

2) _____

3) _____

TODAY'S MINDFUL ACTIVITY

When I brush my teeth, I'm just going to brush my teeth. Nothing else... besides noticing all there is to brushing my teeth and taking care of myself in this way.

_____

(or my choice of Mindful Activity)

PEACEFUL PAUSES   🐾 🐾 🐾 🐾 🐾 🐾 🐾 🐾 🐾

_____

(my Peaceful Pause activity)

86

BODY CARE

Hydration

Veggies

"My-Body-Thanks-Me" Foods

_____

Exercise &
Movement: _____
                                             (time and activity)

Today's appreciation for my body:
_____

TODAY'S REFLECTION

What did I do well today?

_____

_____

_____

What did I learn from a challenging moment?

_____

_____

Three words to celebrate me today: _____

Fortune favors the Bold.

~ Terrence

WAKING UP   DAY 2   Date _____

Today I feel:

_____

My Happiness Scale 1 - 10 _____   I slept _____ hours

I'm looking forward to:

_____

My intention for the day:

_____

SELF-CARE   3 ways I'm going to care for myself:

1) _____

2) _____

3) _____

TODAY'S MINDFUL ACTIVITY

When I brush my teeth, I'm just going to brush my teeth. Nothing else... besides noticing all there is to brushing my teeth and taking care of myself in this way.

(or my choice of Mindful Activity)

PEACEFUL PAUSES   🐾 🐾 🐾 🐾 🐾 🐾 🐾 🐾 🐾

(my Peaceful Pause activity)

BODY CARE

Hydration

Veggies

"My-Body-Thanks-Me" Foods

_____

Exercise &
Movement: _____

(time and activity)

Today's appreciation for my body:

_____

TODAY'S REFLECTION

What did I do well today?

_____

_____

_____

What did I learn from a challenging moment?

_____

_____

Three words to celebrate me today: _____

The curious paradox is that when I accept myself as I am, then I can change.

~ Carl Rogers

WAKING UP   **DAY 3**   Date _____

Today I feel:

_____

My Happiness Scale 1 - 10 _____   I slept _____ hours

I'm looking forward to:

_____

My intention for the day:

_____

SELF-CARE   3 ways I'm going to care for myself:

1) _____

2) _____

3) _____

TODAY'S MINDFUL ACTIVITY

When I brush my teeth, I'm just going to brush my teeth. Nothing else... besides noticing all there is to brushing my teeth and taking care of myself in this way.

_____
(or my choice of Mindful Activity)

PEACEFUL PAUSES   🐾 🐾 🐾 🐾 🐾 🐾 🐾 🐾 🐾

_____
(my Peaceful Pause activity)

BODY CARE

Hydration

Veggies

"My-Body-Thanks-Me" Foods

_____

Exercise &
Movement: _____
(time and activity)

Today's appreciation for my body:

_____

TODAY'S REFLECTION

What did I do well today?

_____

_____

_____

What did I learn from a challenging moment?

_____

_____

_____

Three words to celebrate me today: _____

Restlessness and discontent are
the necessities of progress.

~ Thomas Edison

WAKING UP   DAY 4   Date _____

Today I feel:

_____

My Happiness Scale 1 - 10 _____   I slept _____ hours

I'm looking forward to:

_____

My intention for the day:

_____

SELF-CARE   3 ways I'm going to care for myself:

1) _____

2) _____

3) _____

TODAY'S MINDFUL ACTIVITY

When I brush my teeth, I'm just going to brush my teeth. Nothing else... besides noticing all there is to brushing my teeth and taking care of myself in this way.

_____
(or my choice of Mindful Activity)

PEACEFUL PAUSES   🐾 🐾 🐾 🐾 🐾 🐾 🐾 🐾 🐾 🐾

_____
(my Peaceful Pause activity)

BODY CARE

Hydration 🌢🌢🌢🌢🌢
🌢🌢🌢🌢🌢

Veggies

"My-Body-Thanks-Me" Foods

_____

Exercise & Movement: _____

(time and activity)

Today's appreciation for my body:

_____

TODAY'S REFLECTION

What did I do well today?

_____

_____

_____

What did I learn from a challenging moment?

_____

_____

_____

Three words to celebrate me today: _____

Courage is like a muscle.
We strengthen it by use.

~ Ruth Gordon

WAKING UP   **DAY 5**   Date _____

Today I feel:

_____

My Happiness Scale 1 - 10 _____   I slept _____ hours

I'm looking forward to:

_____

My intention for the day:

_____

SELF-CARE   3 ways I'm going to care for myself:

1) _____

2) _____

3) _____

TODAY'S MINDFUL ACTIVITY

When I brush my teeth, I'm just going to brush my teeth. Nothing else... besides noticing all there is to brushing my teeth and taking care of myself in this way.

_____
(or my choice of Mindful Activity)

PEACEFUL PAUSES   🐾 🐾 🐾 🐾 🐾 🐾 🐾 🐾 🐾

_____
(my Peaceful Pause activity)

94

BODY CARE

Hydration

Veggies

"My-Body-Thanks-Me" Foods

_____

Exercise &
Movement:

(time and activity)

Today's appreciation for my body:

_____

TODAY'S REFLECTION

What did I do well today?

_____

_____

_____

What did I learn from a challenging moment?

_____

_____

_____

Three words to celebrate me today: _____

Because of your smile,
you make life more beautiful.

~ Thich Nhat Hanh

WAKING UP **DAY 6** Date _____

Today I feel:

_____

My Happiness Scale 1 - 10 _____ I slept _____ hours

I'm looking forward to:

_____

My intention for the day:

_____

SELF-CARE 3 ways I'm going to care for myself:

1) _____

2) _____

3) _____

TODAY'S MINDFUL ACTIVITY

When I brush my teeth, I'm just going to brush my teeth. Nothing else... besides noticing all there is to brushing my teeth and taking care of myself in this way.

_____

(or my choice of Mindful Activity)

PEACEFUL PAUSES 🐾 🐾 🐾 🐾 🐾 🐾 🐾 🐾 🐾 🐾

_____

(my Peaceful Pause activity)

BODY CARE

Hydration

Veggies

"My-Body-Thanks-Me" Foods

_____

Exercise &
Movement:

(time and activity)

Today's appreciation for my body:

_____

TODAY'S REFLECTION

What did I do well today?

_____

_____

_____

What did I learn from a challenging moment?

_____

_____

_____

Three words to celebrate me today: _____

Against the assault of laughter
nothing can stand.

~ Mark Twain

WAKING UP   **DAY 7**   Date _____

Today I feel:

_____

My Happiness Scale 1 - 10 _____   I slept _____ hours

I'm looking forward to:

_____

My intention for the day:

_____

SELF-CARE   3 ways I'm going to care for myself:

1) _____

2) _____

3) _____

TODAY'S MINDFUL ACTIVITY

When I brush my teeth, I'm just going to brush my teeth. Nothing else... besides noticing all there is to brushing my teeth and taking care of myself in this way.

_____
(or my choice of Mindful Activity)

PEACEFUL PAUSES   🐾 🐾 🐾 🐾 🐾 🐾 🐾 🐾 🐾

_____
(my Peaceful Pause activity)

98

BODY CARE

Hydration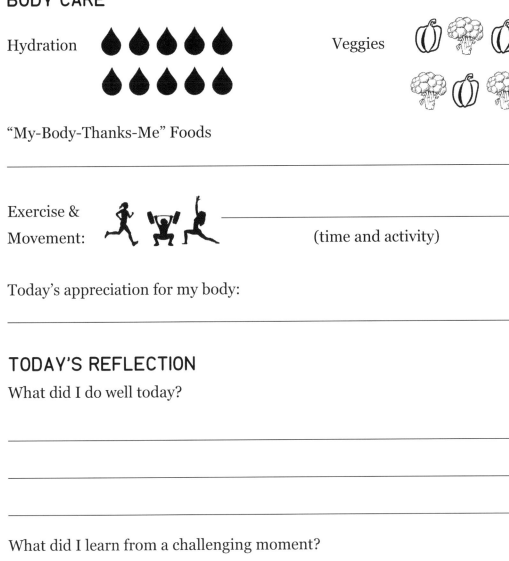

Veggies

"My-Body-Thanks-Me" Foods

_____

Exercise &
Movement: _____

(time and activity)

Today's appreciation for my body:

_____

TODAY'S REFLECTION

What did I do well today?

_____

_____

_____

What did I learn from a challenging moment?

_____

_____

_____

Three words to celebrate me today: _____

These are all the things that bring me joy.

Enjoy a few moments of meditation

To access, please go to http://bit.ly/EverydayEaseMeditations

FREE SPACE for journaling and reflection

And the day came when the risk to remain
tight in a bud was more painful
than the risk took to blossom. ~ Anais Nin

WAKING UP   DAY 8   Date _____

Today I feel:

_____

My Happiness Scale 1 - 10 _____   I slept _____ hours

I'm looking forward to:

_____

My intention for the day:

_____

SELF—CARE   3 ways I'm going to care for myself:

1) _____

2) _____

3) _____

TODAY'S MINDFUL ACTIVITY

Washing my hands helps me come back to the clean and clear present moment.

_____
(or my choice of Mindful Activity)

PEACEFUL PAUSES   🐾 🐾 🐾 🐾 🐾 🐾 🐾 🐾 🐾

_____
(my Peaceful Pause activity)

BODY CARE

Hydration

Veggies

"My-Body-Thanks-Me" Foods

_____

Exercise &
Movement: (time and activity)

Today's appreciation for my body:

_____

TODAY'S REFLECTION

What did I do well today?

_____

_____

_____

What did I learn from a challenging moment?

_____

_____

_____

Three words to celebrate me today: _____

Happiness is when what you think, what you say, and what you do are in harmony.

~ Mahatma Ghandi

WAKING UP **DAY 9** Date _____

Today I feel:

_____

My Happiness Scale 1 - 10 _____ I slept _____ hours

I'm looking forward to:

_____

My intention for the day:

_____

SELF-CARE 3 ways I'm going to care for myself:

1) _____

2) _____

3) _____

TODAY'S MINDFUL ACTIVITY

Washing my hands helps me come back to the clean and clear present moment.

_____

(or my choice of Mindful Activity)

PEACEFUL PAUSES 🐾 🐾 🐾 🐾 🐾 🐾 🐾 🐾 🐾

_____

(my Peaceful Pause activity)

BODY CARE

Hydration

Veggies

"My-Body-Thanks-Me" Foods

_____

Exercise &
Movement: (time and activity)

Today's appreciation for my body:

_____

TODAY'S REFLECTION

What did I do well today?

_____

_____

_____

What did I learn from a challenging moment?

_____

_____

_____

Three words to celebrate me today: _____

105

Clarity is born of persistence and letting go.

~ Shanti Douglas

WAKING UP   DAY 10   Date _____

Today I feel:

_____

My Happiness Scale 1 - 10 _____   I slept _____ hours

I'm looking forward to:

_____

My intention for the day:

_____

SELF-CARE   3 ways I'm going to care for myself:

1) _____

2) _____

3) _____

TODAY'S MINDFUL ACTIVITY

Washing my hands helps me come back to the clean and clear present moment.

_____

(or my choice of Mindful Activity)

PEACEFUL PAUSES   🐾 🐾 🐾 🐾 🐾 🐾 🐾 🐾 🐾 🐾

_____

(my Peaceful Pause activity)

BODY CARE

Hydration ⬤⬤⬤⬤⬤
⬤⬤⬤⬤⬤

Veggies

"My-Body-Thanks-Me" Foods

_____

Exercise & Movement: _____
(time and activity)

Today's appreciation for my body:

_____

TODAY'S REFLECTION

What did I do well today?

_____

_____

_____

What did I learn from a challenging moment?

_____

_____

_____

Three words to celebrate me today: _____

Because you are alive,
everything is possible.

~ Thich Nhat Hanh

WAKING UP   **DAY 11**   Date _____

Today I feel:

_____

My Happiness Scale 1 - 10 _____   I slept _____ hours

I'm looking forward to:

_____

My intention for the day:

_____

SELF-CARE   3 ways I'm going to care for myself:

1) _____

2) _____

3) _____

TODAY'S MINDFUL ACTIVITY

   Washing my hands helps me come back to the clean and clear present moment.

_____

(or my choice of Mindful Activity)

PEACEFUL PAUSES   🐾 🐾 🐾 🐾 🐾 🐾 🐾 🐾 🐾

_____

(my Peaceful Pause activity)

BODY CARE

Hydration

Veggies

"My-Body-Thanks-Me" Foods

_____

Exercise &
Movement: _____
(time and activity)

Today's appreciation for my body:

_____

TODAY'S REFLECTION

What did I do well today?

_____

_____

_____

What did I learn from a challenging moment?

_____

_____

_____

Three words to celebrate me today: _____

It's only those who do nothing who make no mistakes.

~ Joseph Conrad

WAKING UP   **DAY 12**   Date _____

Today I feel:

_____

My Happiness Scale 1 - 10 _____   I slept _____ hours

I'm looking forward to:

_____

My intention for the day:

_____

SELF-CARE   3 ways I'm going to care for myself:

1) _____

2) _____

3) _____

TODAY'S MINDFUL ACTIVITY

    Washing my hands helps me come back to the clean and clear present moment.

_____

(or my choice of Mindful Activity)

PEACEFUL PAUSES   🐾 🐾 🐾 🐾 🐾 🐾 🐾 🐾 🐾

_____

(my Peaceful Pause activity)

110

BODY CARE

Hydration

Veggies

"My-Body-Thanks-Me" Foods

_____

Exercise &
Movement: (time and activity)

Today's appreciation for my body:

_____

TODAY'S REFLECTION

What did I do well today?

_____

_____

_____

What did I learn from a challenging moment?

_____

_____

_____

Three words to celebrate me today: _____

It's your place in the world; it's your life.
Go on and do all you can with it,
and make it the life you want to live.

~ Mae Jamison

WAKING UP DAY 13 Date _____

Today I feel:

_____

My Happiness Scale 1 - 10 _____   I slept _____ hours

I'm looking forward to:

_____

My intention for the day:

_____

SELF-CARE   3 ways I'm going to care for myself:

1) _____

2) _____

3) _____

TODAY'S MINDFUL ACTIVITY

Washing my hands helps me come back to the clean and clear present moment.

_____
(or my choice of Mindful Activity)

PEACEFUL PAUSES 🐾 🐾 🐾 🐾 🐾 🐾 🐾 🐾 🐾 🐾

_____
(my Peaceful Pause activity)

BODY CARE

Hydration

Veggies

"My-Body-Thanks-Me" Foods

_____

Exercise &
Movement: (time and activity)

Today's appreciation for my body:

_____

TODAY'S REFLECTION

What did I do well today?

_____

_____

_____

What did I learn from a challenging moment?

_____

_____

_____

Three words to celebrate me today: _____

When I dare to be powerful, to use my strength in the service of my vision, then it becomes less and less important whether I am afraid.

~ Audre Lorde

WAKING UP
DAY 14
Date _____

Today I feel:

_____

My Happiness Scale 1 - 10 _____   I slept _____ hours

I'm looking forward to:

_____

My intention for the day:

_____

SELF-CARE
3 ways I'm going to care for myself:

1) _____

2) _____

3) _____

TODAY'S MINDFUL ACTIVITY

Washing my hands helps me come back to the clean and clear present moment.

_____

(or my choice of Mindful Activity)

PEACEFUL PAUSES   🐾 🐾 🐾 🐾 🐾 🐾 🐾 🐾 🐾 🐾

_____

(my Peaceful Pause activity)

BODY CARE

Hydration

Veggies

"My-Body-Thanks-Me" Foods

_____

Exercise &
Movement: _____
                                   (time and activity)

Today's appreciation for my body:

_____

TODAY'S REFLECTION

What did I do well today?

_____

_____

_____

What did I learn from a challenging moment?

_____

_____

Three words to celebrate me today: _____

These are all the people that love me. I'm so grateful.

Enjoy a few moments of meditation

To access, please go to http://bit.ly/EverydayEaseMeditations

FREE SPACE for journaling and reflection

Too many of us are not living our dreams because we're living our fears.

~ Les Brown

WAKING UP   DAY 15   Date _____

Today I feel:

_____

My Happiness Scale 1 - 10 _____   I slept _____ hours

I'm looking forward to:

_____

My intention for the day:

_____

SELF-CARE   3 ways I'm going to care for myself:

1) _____

2) _____

3) _____

TODAY'S MINDFUL ACTIVITY

I eat the first 5 minutes of every meal mindfully, being present to the food and myself.

_____

(or my choice of Mindful Activity)

PEACEFUL PAUSES   🐾 🐾 🐾 🐾 🐾 🐾 🐾 🐾 🐾 🐾

_____

(my Peaceful Pause activity)

BODY CARE

Hydration

Veggies

"My-Body-Thanks-Me" Foods

_____

Exercise &
Movement: _____
                                             (time and activity)

Today's appreciation for my body:

_____

TODAY'S REFLECTION

What did I do well today?

_____

_____

_____

What did I learn from a challenging moment?

_____

_____

_____

Three words to celebrate me today: _____

It's not the load that breaks you down... it's the way you carry it.

~ Lena Horne

WAKING UP   DAY 16   Date _____

Today I feel:

_____

My Happiness Scale 1 - 10 _____   I slept _____ hours

I'm looking forward to:

_____

My intention for the day:

_____

SELF-CARE   3 ways I'm going to care for myself:

1) _____

2) _____

3) _____

TODAY'S MINDFUL ACTIVITY

I eat the first 5 minutes of every meal mindfully, being present to the food and myself.

_____

(or my choice of Mindful Activity)

PEACEFUL PAUSES   🐾 🐾 🐾 🐾 🐾 🐾 🐾 🐾 🐾

_____

(my Peaceful Pause activity)

120

BODY CARE

Hydration ⬛💧💧💧💧💧 💧💧💧💧💧

Veggies

"My-Body-Thanks-Me" Foods

_____

Exercise &
Movement: _____
(time and activity)

Today's appreciation for my body:

_____

TODAY'S REFLECTION

What did I do well today?

_____

_____

_____

What did I learn from a challenging moment?

_____

_____

_____

Three words to celebrate me today: _____

Half an hour's meditation each day is essential, except when you are busy. Then a full hour is needed.

~ St. Francis de Sales

WAKING UP   DAY 17   Date _____

Today I feel:

_____

My Happiness Scale 1 - 10 _____   I slept _____ hours

I'm looking forward to:

_____

My intention for the day:

_____

SELF-CARE   3 ways I'm going to care for myself:

1) _____

2) _____

3) _____

TODAY'S MINDFUL ACTIVITY

I eat the first 5 minutes of every meal mindfully, being present to the food and myself.

_____

(or my choice of Mindful Activity)

PEACEFUL PAUSES   🐾 🐾 🐾 🐾 🐾 🐾 🐾 🐾 🐾

_____

(my Peaceful Pause activity)

BODY CARE

Hydration

Veggies

"My-Body-Thanks-Me" Foods

_____

Exercise &
Movement: _____
                                             (time and activity)

Today's appreciation for my body:

_____

TODAY'S REFLECTION

What did I do well today?

_____

_____

_____

What did I learn from a challenging moment?

_____

_____

_____

Three words to celebrate me today: _____

Optimism is true moral courage.

~ Ernest Shackleton

WAKING UP   **DAY 18**   Date _____

Today I feel:

_____

My Happiness Scale 1 - 10 _____   I slept _____ hours

I'm looking forward to:

_____

My intention for the day:

_____

SELF-CARE   3 ways I'm going to care for myself:

1) _____

2) _____

3) _____

TODAY'S MINDFUL ACTIVITY

I eat the first 5 minutes of every meal mindfully, being present to the food and myself.

_____

(or my choice of Mindful Activity)

PEACEFUL PAUSES   🐾 🐾 🐾 🐾 🐾 🐾 🐾 🐾 🐾 🐾

_____

(my Peaceful Pause activity)

BODY CARE

Hydration ●●●●●
●●●●●

Veggies

"My-Body-Thanks-Me" Foods

_____

Exercise &
Movement: _____
(time and activity)

Today's appreciation for my body:

_____

TODAY'S REFLECTION

What did I do well today?

_____

_____

_____

What did I learn from a challenging moment?

_____

_____

_____

Three words to celebrate me today: _____

Wellbeing is attained little by little, and nevertheless it is no little thing.

~ Zeno

WAKING UP   DAY 19   Date _____

Today I feel:

_____

My Happiness Scale 1 - 10 _____   I slept _____ hours

I'm looking forward to:

_____

My intention for the day:

_____

SELF-CARE   3 ways I'm going to care for myself:

1) _____

2) _____

3) _____

TODAY'S MINDFUL ACTIVITY

I eat the first 5 minutes of every meal mindfully, being present to the food and myself.

_____

(or my choice of Mindful Activity)

PEACEFUL PAUSES   🐾 🐾 🐾 🐾 🐾 🐾 🐾 🐾 🐾 🐾

_____

(my Peaceful Pause activity)

BODY CARE

Hydration

Veggies

"My-Body-Thanks-Me" Foods

_____

Exercise &
Movement: (time and activity)

Today's appreciation for my body:

_____

TODAY'S REFLECTION

What did I do well today?

_____

_____

_____

What did I learn from a challenging moment?

_____

_____

_____

Three words to celebrate me today: _____

We think more of extending life than of filling it.

~ Tomas Masaryk

WAKING UP   **DAY 20**   Date _____

Today I feel:

_____

My Happiness Scale 1 - 10 _____   I slept _____ hours

I'm looking forward to:

_____

My intention for the day:

_____

SELF-CARE   3 ways I'm going to care for myself:

1) _____

2) _____

3) _____

TODAY'S MINDFUL ACTIVITY

I eat the first 5 minutes of every meal mindfully, being present to the food and myself.

_____

(or my choice of Mindful Activity)

PEACEFUL PAUSES   🐾 🐾 🐾 🐾 🐾 🐾 🐾 🐾 🐾

_____

(my Peaceful Pause activity)

BODY CARE

Hydration

Veggies

"My-Body-Thanks-Me" Foods

_____

Exercise &
Movement: _____

(time and activity)

Today's appreciation for my body:

_____

TODAY'S REFLECTION

What did I do well today?

_____

_____

_____

What did I learn from a challenging moment?

_____

_____

_____

Three words to celebrate me today: _____

Your willingness to look at your darkness is what empowers you to change.

~ Iyanla Vanzant

WAKING UP   **DAY 21**   Date _____

Today I feel:

_____

My Happiness Scale 1 - 10 _____   I slept _____ hours

I'm looking forward to:

_____

My intention for the day:

_____

SELF-CARE   3 ways I'm going to care for myself:

1) _____

2) _____

3) _____

TODAY'S MINDFUL ACTIVITY

I eat the first 5 minutes of every meal mindfully, being present to the food and myself.

_____

(or my choice of Mindful Activity)

PEACEFUL PAUSES   🐾 🐾 🐾 🐾 🐾 🐾 🐾 🐾 🐾

_____

(my Peaceful Pause activity)

BODY CARE

Hydration ⬛💧💧💧💧💧💧💧💧💧   Veggies

"My-Body-Thanks-Me" Foods

_____

Exercise &
Movement: _____
                                                    (time and activity)

Today's appreciation for my body:

_____

TODAY'S REFLECTION

What did I do well today?

_____

_____

_____

What did I learn from a challenging moment?

_____

_____

_____

Three words to celebrate me today: _____

look down at your body
whisper
there's no home like you
thank you

~ Rupi Kaur ~

Draw an outline of your beautiful body and fill it with flowers, smiles, rays of sunshine, moons, trees, music notes, butterflies, happy faces, hearts, prayers flags, colors, birds, grasses, mountains, muscles,... whatever feels fitting and wonderful.

Enjoy a few moments of meditation

To access, please go to http://bit.ly/EverydayEaseMeditations

FREE SPACE for journaling and reflection

What you think, you become.

WAKING UP   **DAY 22**   Date _____

Today I feel:

_____

My Happiness Scale 1 - 10 _____   I slept _____ hours

I'm looking forward to:

_____

My intention for the day:

_____

SELF-CARE   3 ways I'm going to care for myself:

1) _____

2) _____

3) _____

TODAY'S MINDFUL ACTIVITY

Walking _____ (this place), I'll bring my mind
        and body together to notice my steps, staying grounded in the walking.

_____

(or my choice of Mindful Activity)

PEACEFUL PAUSES   🐾 🐾 🐾 🐾 🐾 🐾 🐾 🐾 🐾

_____

(my Peaceful Pause activity)

134

BODY CARE

Hydration

Veggies

"My-Body-Thanks-Me" Foods

_____

Exercise & Movement: _____

(time and activity)

Today's appreciation for my body:

_____

TODAY'S REFLECTION

What did I do well today?

_____

_____

_____

What did I learn from a challenging moment?

_____

_____

_____

Three words to celebrate me today: _____

Peace in oneself.
Peace in the world.

~ Thich Nhat Hanh

WAKING UP   DAY 23   Date _____

Today I feel:

_____

My Happiness Scale 1 - 10 _____   I slept _____ hours

I'm looking forward to:

_____

My intention for the day:

_____

SELF-CARE   3 ways I'm going to care for myself:

1) _____

2) _____

3) _____

TODAY'S MINDFUL ACTIVITY

Walking _____ (this place), I'll bring my mind
and body together to notice my steps, staying grounded in the walking.

_____

(or my choice of Mindful Activity)

PEACEFUL PAUSES   🐾 🐾 🐾 🐾 🐾 🐾 🐾 🐾 🐾

_____

(my Peaceful Pause activity)

BODY CARE

Hydration ●●●●● ●●●●●

Veggies

"My-Body-Thanks-Me" Foods

_____

Exercise &
Movement: _____

(time and activity)

Today's appreciation for my body:

_____

TODAY'S REFLECTION

What did I do well today?

_____

_____

_____

What did I learn from a challenging moment?

_____

_____

_____

Three words to celebrate me today: _____

There's a crack in everything.
That's how the light gets in.

~ Leonard Cohen

WAKING UP

DAY 24

Date _____

Today I feel:

_____

My Happiness Scale 1 - 10 _____

I slept _____ hours

I'm looking forward to:

_____

My intention for the day:

_____

SELF-CARE

3 ways I'm going to care for myself:

1) _____

2) _____

3) _____

TODAY'S MINDFUL ACTIVITY

Walking _____ (this place), I'll bring my mind
and body together to notice my steps, staying grounded in the walking.

_____

(or my choice of Mindful Activity)

PEACEFUL PAUSES

🐾 🐾 🐾 🐾 🐾 🐾 🐾 🐾 🐾 🐾

_____

(my Peaceful Pause activity)

BODY CARE

Hydration

Veggies

"My-Body-Thanks-Me" Foods

_____

Exercise &
Movement: _____
(time and activity)

Today's appreciation for my body:

_____

TODAY'S REFLECTION

What did I do well today?

_____

_____

_____

What did I learn from a challenging moment?

_____

_____

_____

Three words to celebrate me today: _____

If someone doesn't care about himself, you begin to lose interest after a while.

~ Kem Nunn

WAKING UP   **DAY 25**   Date _____

Today I feel:

_____

My Happiness Scale 1 - 10 _____   I slept _____ hours

I'm looking forward to:

_____

My intention for the day:

_____

SELF-CARE   3 ways I'm going to care for myself:

1) _____

2) _____

3) _____

TODAY'S MINDFUL ACTIVITY

Walking _____ (this place), I'll bring my mind
and body together to notice my steps, staying grounded in the walking.

_____

(or my choice of Mindful Activity)

PEACEFUL PAUSES   🐾 🐾 🐾 🐾 🐾 🐾 🐾 🐾 🐾

_____

(my Peaceful Pause activity)

140

BODY CARE

Hydration

Veggies

"My-Body-Thanks-Me" Foods

_____

Exercise &
Movement: (time and activity)

Today's appreciation for my body:

_____

TODAY'S REFLECTION

What did I do well today?

_____

_____

_____

What did I learn from a challenging moment?

_____

_____

_____

Three words to celebrate me today: _____

The misfortunes hardest to bear
are those which never happen.

~ James Russell Lowell

WAKING UP   DAY 26   Date _____

Today I feel:

_____

My Happiness Scale 1 - 10 _____   I slept _____ hours

I'm looking forward to:

_____

My intention for the day:

_____

SELF-CARE   3 ways I'm going to care for myself:

1) _____

2) _____

3) _____

TODAY'S MINDFUL ACTIVITY

Walking _____ (this place), I'll bring my mind
and body together to notice my steps, staying grounded in the walking.

_____

(or my choice of Mindful Activity)

PEACEFUL PAUSES   🐾 🐾 🐾 🐾 🐾 🐾 🐾 🐾 🐾 🐾

_____

(my Peaceful Pause activity)

BODY CARE

Hydration ●●●●●
●●●●●

Veggies

"My-Body-Thanks-Me" Foods

_____

Exercise &
Movement:
_____
(time and activity)

Today's appreciation for my body:

_____

TODAY'S REFLECTION

What did I do well today?

_____

_____

_____

What did I learn from a challenging moment?

_____

_____

_____

Three words to celebrate me today: _____

If there is to be any peace it will come through being, not having.

~ Henry Miller

WAKING UP   DAY 27   Date _____

Today I feel:

_____

My Happiness Scale 1 - 10 _____   I slept _____ hours

I'm looking forward to:

_____

My intention for the day:

_____

SELF-CARE   3 ways I'm going to care for myself:

1) _____

2) _____

3) _____

TODAY'S MINDFUL ACTIVITY

Walking _____ (this place), I'll bring my mind
and body together to notice my steps, staying grounded in the walking.

_____

(or my choice of Mindful Activity)

PEACEFUL PAUSES   🐾 🐾 🐾 🐾 🐾 🐾 🐾 🐾 🐾 🐾

_____

(my Peaceful Pause activity)

144

BODY CARE

Hydration

Veggies

"My-Body-Thanks-Me" Foods

_____

Exercise &
Movement: _____
                                       (time and activity)

Today's appreciation for my body:

_____

TODAY'S REFLECTION

What did I do well today?

_____

_____

_____

What did I learn from a challenging moment?

_____

_____

Three words to celebrate me today: _____

The best thing one can do when it's raining is to let it rain.

~ Henry Wadsworth Longfellow

WAKING UP   DAY 28   Date _____

Today I feel:

_____

My Happiness Scale 1 - 10 _____   I slept _____ hours

I'm looking forward to:

_____

My intention for the day:

_____

SELF-CARE   3 ways I'm going to care for myself:

1) _____

2) _____

3) _____

TODAY'S MINDFUL ACTIVITY

Walking _____ (this place), I'll bring my mind
and body together to notice my steps, staying grounded in the walking.

_____

(or my choice of Mindful Activity)

PEACEFUL PAUSES   🐾 🐾 🐾 🐾 🐾 🐾 🐾 🐾 🐾

_____

(my Peaceful Pause activity)

BODY CARE

Hydration

Veggies

"My-Body-Thanks-Me" Foods

_____

Exercise &
Movement: _____

                                    (time and activity)

Today's appreciation for my body:

_____

TODAY'S REFLECTION

What did I do well today?

_____

_____

_____

What did I learn from a challenging moment?

_____

_____

_____

Three words to celebrate me today: _____

Spend a few minutes looking into a mirror.
What inner and outer beauty do you see?

Enjoy a few moments of meditation

To access, please go to http://bit.ly/EverydayEaseMeditations

FREE SPACE for journaling and reflection

Suffering comes when we seek happiness beyond this moment.

~ Shanti Douglas

WAKING UP   DAY 29   Date _____

Today I feel:

_____

My Happiness Scale 1 - 10 _____   I slept _____ hours

I'm looking forward to:

_____

My intention for the day:

_____

SELF-CARE   3 ways I'm going to care for myself:

1) _____

2) _____

3) _____

TODAY'S MINDFUL ACTIVITY

Stop signs and stop lights remind me to stop and come back to myself.

_____

(or my choice of Mindful Activity)

PEACEFUL PAUSES   🐾 🐾 🐾 🐾 🐾 🐾 🐾 🐾 🐾 🐾

_____

(my Peaceful Pause activity)

BODY CARE

Hydration ⬥ ⬥ ⬥ ⬥ ⬥
⬥ ⬥ ⬥ ⬥ ⬥

Veggies

"My-Body-Thanks-Me" Foods

_____

Exercise &
Movement:

_____
(time and activity)

Today's appreciation for my body:

_____

TODAY'S REFLECTION

What did I do well today?

_____

_____

_____

What did I learn from a challenging moment?

_____

_____

_____

Three words to celebrate me today: _____

> *Just when the caterpillar thought her life was over, she became a butterfly.*
>
> ~ Bess Gallanis

WAKING UP   DAY 30   Date _____

Today I feel:

_____

My Happiness Scale 1 - 10 _____   I slept _____ hours

I'm looking forward to:

_____

My intention for the day:

_____

SELF-CARE   3 ways I'm going to care for myself:

1) _____

2) _____

3) _____

TODAY'S MINDFUL ACTIVITY

Stop signs and stop lights remind me to stop and come back to myself.

_____

(or my choice of Mindful Activity)

PEACEFUL PAUSES 🐾 🐾 🐾 🐾 🐾 🐾 🐾 🐾 🐾

_____

(my Peaceful Pause activity)

152

BODY CARE

Hydration

Veggies

"My-Body-Thanks-Me" Foods

_____

Exercise &
Movement: (time and activity)

Today's appreciation for my body:

_____

TODAY'S REFLECTION

What did I do well today?

_____

_____

_____

What did I learn from a challenging moment?

_____

_____

_____

Three words to celebrate me today: _____

You may not be what you think you are
but what you think, you are.

~ Jim Clark

WAKING UP   DAY 31   Date _____

Today I feel:

_____

My Happiness Scale 1 - 10 _____   I slept _____ hours

I'm looking forward to:

_____

My intention for the day:

_____

SELF-CARE   3 ways I'm going to care for myself:

1) _____

2) _____

3) _____

TODAY'S MINDFUL ACTIVITY

Stop signs and stop lights remind me to stop and come back to myself.

_____

(or my choice of Mindful Activity)

PEACEFUL PAUSES   🐾 🐾 🐾 🐾 🐾 🐾 🐾 🐾 🐾

_____

(my Peaceful Pause activity)

BODY CARE

Hydration

Veggies

"My-Body-Thanks-Me" Foods

_____

Exercise &
Movement: _____

(time and activity)

Today's appreciation for my body:

_____

TODAY'S REFLECTION

What did I do well today?

_____

_____

_____

What did I learn from a challenging moment?

_____

_____

_____

Three words to celebrate me today: _____

The only change you can make to your past is your perception.

~ Shanti Douglas

WAKING UP   DAY 32   Date _____

Today I feel:

_____

My Happiness Scale 1 - 10 _____   I slept _____ hours

I'm looking forward to:

_____

My intention for the day:

_____

SELF-CARE   3 ways I'm going to care for myself:

1) _____

2) _____

3) _____

TODAY'S MINDFUL ACTIVITY

Stop signs and stop lights remind me to stop and come back to myself.

_____

(or my choice of Mindful Activity)

PEACEFUL PAUSES   🐾 🐾 🐾 🐾 🐾 🐾 🐾 🐾 🐾

_____

(my Peaceful Pause activity)

BODY CARE

Hydration

Veggies

"My-Body-Thanks-Me" Foods

_____

Exercise &
Movement: _____
                             (time and activity)

Today's appreciation for my body:

_____

TODAY'S REFLECTION

What did I do well today?

_____

_____

_____

What did I learn from a challenging moment?

_____

_____

_____

Three words to celebrate me today: _____

That which has roots will endure.

~ Anodeau Judith, PhD.

WAKING UP   DAY 33   Date _____

Today I feel:

_____

My Happiness Scale 1 - 10 _____   I slept _____ hours

I'm looking forward to:

_____

My intention for the day:

_____

SELF-CARE   3 ways I'm going to care for myself:

1) _____

2) _____

3) _____

TODAY'S MINDFUL ACTIVITY

Stop signs and stop lights remind me to stop and come back to myself.

_____

(or my choice of Mindful Activity)

PEACEFUL PAUSES   🐾 🐾 🐾 🐾 🐾 🐾 🐾 🐾 🐾 🐾

_____

(my Peaceful Pause activity)

BODY CARE

Hydration

Veggies

"My-Body-Thanks-Me" Foods

_____

Exercise &
Movement:

_____
(time and activity)

Today's appreciation for my body:

_____

TODAY'S REFLECTION

What did I do well today?

_____

_____

_____

What did I learn from a challenging moment?

_____

_____

Three words to celebrate me today: _____

One does not become enlightened
by imagining figures of light,
but by making the darkness conscious.

~ CG Jung

WAKING UP   DAY 34   Date _____

Today I feel:

_____

My Happiness Scale 1 - 10 _____   I slept _____ hours

I'm looking forward to:

_____

My intention for the day:

_____

SELF–CARE   3 ways I'm going to care for myself:

1) _____

2) _____

3) _____

TODAY'S MINDFUL ACTIVITY

Stop signs and stop lights remind me to stop and come back to myself.

_____

(or my choice of Mindful Activity)

PEACEFUL PAUSES   🐾 🐾 🐾 🐾 🐾 🐾 🐾 🐾 🐾 🐾

_____

(my Peaceful Pause activity)

BODY CARE

Hydration

Veggies

"My-Body-Thanks-Me" Foods

_____

Exercise &
Movement:

_____
(time and activity)

Today's appreciation for my body:

_____

TODAY'S REFLECTION

What did I do well today?

_____

_____

_____

What did I learn from a challenging moment?

_____

_____

_____

Three words to celebrate me today: _____

*The essence of bravery is
being without self-deception.*

~ Pema Chodron

WAKING UP   DAY 35   Date _____

Today I feel:

_____

My Happiness Scale 1 - 10 _____   I slept _____ hours

I'm looking forward to:

_____

My intention for the day:

_____

SELF–CARE   3 ways I'm going to care for myself:

1) _____

2) _____

3) _____

TODAY'S MINDFUL ACTIVITY

Stop signs and stop lights remind me to stop and come back to myself.

_____

(or my choice of Mindful Activity)

PEACEFUL PAUSES   🐾 🐾 🐾 🐾 🐾 🐾 🐾 🐾 🐾

_____

(my Peaceful Pause activity)

162

BODY CARE

Hydration

Veggies

"My-Body-Thanks-Me" Foods

_____

Exercise & Movement: _____

(time and activity)

Today's appreciation for my body:

_____

TODAY'S REFLECTION

What did I do well today?

_____

_____

_____

What did I learn from a challenging moment?

_____

_____

_____

Three words to celebrate me today: _____

Balance and ease can come from many places. What are 3 places that provide a sense of balance and ease for you?
Put them in the flower petals below then surround them with warm colors, words, or other graphics.

Enjoy a few moments of meditation

To access, please go to http://bit.ly/EverydayEaseMeditations

FREE SPACE for journaling and reflection

Friendship with oneself is all important,
because without it one cannot be friends
with anyone else in the world.

~ Eleanor Roosevelt

WAKING UP
DAY 36
Date _____

Today I feel:

_____

My Happiness Scale 1 - 10 _____   I slept _____ hours

I'm looking forward to:

_____

My intention for the day:

_____

SELF-CARE   3 ways I'm going to care for myself:

1) _____

2) _____

3) _____

TODAY'S MINDFUL ACTIVITY

I shower my body with love, gratitude, and kindness.

_____

(or my choice of Mindful Activity)

PEACEFUL PAUSES   🐾 🐾 🐾 🐾 🐾 🐾 🐾 🐾 🐾

_____

(my Peaceful Pause activity)

BODY CARE

Hydration

●●●●●
●●●●●

Veggies

"My-Body-Thanks-Me" Foods

_____

Exercise &
Movement:

(time and activity)

Today's appreciation for my body:

_____

TODAY'S REFLECTION

What did I do well today?

_____

_____

_____

What did I learn from a challenging moment?

_____

_____

_____

Three words to celebrate me today: _____

Enlightenment is absolute cooperation with the inevitable.

~ Anthony deMello

WAKING UP   **DAY 37**   Date _____

Today I feel:

_____

My Happiness Scale 1 - 10 _____   I slept _____ hours

I'm looking forward to:

_____

My intention for the day:

_____

SELF-CARE   3 ways I'm going to care for myself:

1) _____

2) _____

3) _____

TODAY'S MINDFUL ACTIVITY

I shower my body with love, gratitude, and kindness.

_____

(or my choice of Mindful Activity)

PEACEFUL PAUSES   🐾 🐾 🐾 🐾 🐾 🐾 🐾 🐾 🐾

_____

(my Peaceful Pause activity)

BODY CARE

Hydration

Veggies

"My-Body-Thanks-Me" Foods

_____

Exercise &
Movement:

_____
(time and activity)

Today's appreciation for my body:

_____

TODAY'S REFLECTION

What did I do well today?

_____

_____

_____

What did I learn from a challenging moment?

_____

_____

_____

Three words to celebrate me today: _____

We can't all do great things, but we can all do small things with great love.

~ Mother Theresa

WAKING UP **DAY 38** Date _____

Today I feel:

_____

My Happiness Scale 1 - 10 _____ I slept _____ hours

I'm looking forward to:

_____

My intention for the day:

_____

SELF-CARE 3 ways I'm going to care for myself:

1) _____

2) _____

3) _____

TODAY'S MINDFUL ACTIVITY

I shower my body with love, gratitude, and kindness.

_____

(or my choice of Mindful Activity)

PEACEFUL PAUSES 🐾 🐾 🐾 🐾 🐾 🐾 🐾 🐾 🐾 🐾

_____

(my Peaceful Pause activity)

BODY CARE

Hydration ⬛ ⬛ ⬛ ⬛ ⬛ Veggies

⬛ ⬛ ⬛ ⬛ ⬛

"My-Body-Thanks-Me" Foods

_____

Exercise &

Movement: _____

(time and activity)

Today's appreciation for my body:

_____

TODAY'S REFLECTION

What did I do well today?

_____

_____

_____

What did I learn from a challenging moment?

_____

_____

_____

Three words to celebrate me today: _____

Once you make a decision, the universe conspires to make it happen.

~ Ralph Waldo Emerson

WAKING UP　　　　　　　**DAY 39**　　　　　Date _____

Today I feel:

_____

My Happiness Scale 1 - 10 _____　　　　I slept _____ hours

I'm looking forward to:

_____

My intention for the day:

_____

SELF-CARE　　　　3 ways I'm going to care for myself:

1) _____

2) _____

3) _____

TODAY'S MINDFUL ACTIVITY

I shower my body with love, gratitude, and kindness.

_____

(or my choice of Mindful Activity)

PEACEFUL PAUSES　　🐾 🐾 🐾 🐾 🐾 🐾 🐾 🐾 🐾

_____

(my Peaceful Pause activity)

172

BODY CARE

Hydration

Veggies

"My-Body-Thanks-Me" Foods

_____

Exercise &
Movement:

(time and activity)

Today's appreciation for my body:

_____

TODAY'S REFLECTION

What did I do well today?

_____

_____

_____

What did I learn from a challenging moment?

_____

_____

_____

Three words to celebrate me today: _____

If people truly love you, they want to understand who you are, not prune who you are.

~ Mark Nepo

WAKING UP   **DAY 40**   Date _____

Today I feel:

_____

My Happiness Scale 1 - 10 _____   I slept _____ hours

I'm looking forward to:

_____

My intention for the day:

_____

SELF-CARE   3 ways I'm going to care for myself:

1) _____

2) _____

3) _____

TODAY'S MINDFUL ACTIVITY

I shower my body with love, gratitude, and kindness.

_____

(or my choice of Mindful Activity)

PEACEFUL PAUSES   🐾 🐾 🐾 🐾 🐾 🐾 🐾 🐾 🐾

_____

(my Peaceful Pause activity)

174

BODY CARE

Hydration

Veggies

"My-Body-Thanks-Me" Foods

_____

Exercise &
Movement:

(time and activity)

Today's appreciation for my body:

_____

TODAY'S REFLECTION

What did I do well today?

_____

_____

_____

What did I learn from a challenging moment?

_____

_____

Three words to celebrate me today: _____

Teachers open the door,
but you must enter by yourself.

~ Chinese Proverb

WAKING UP   DAY 41   Date _____

Today I feel:

_____

My Happiness Scale 1 - 10 _____   I slept _____ hours

I'm looking forward to:

_____

My intention for the day:

_____

SELF—CARE   3 ways I'm going to care for myself:

1) _____

2) _____

3) _____

TODAY'S MINDFUL ACTIVITY

I shower my body with love, gratitude, and kindness.

_____

(or my choice of Mindful Activity)

PEACEFUL PAUSES   🐾 🐾 🐾 🐾 🐾 🐾 🐾 🐾 🐾 🐾

_____

(my Peaceful Pause activity)

BODY CARE

Hydration

Veggies

"My-Body-Thanks-Me" Foods

_____

Exercise &
Movement: _____
                                         (time and activity)

Today's appreciation for my body:

_____

TODAY'S REFLECTION

What did I do well today?

_____

_____

_____

What did I learn from a challenging moment?

_____

_____

_____

Three words to celebrate me today: _____

Life happens at the speed of trust.

~ Cheryl Leitschuh

WAKING UP   DAY 42   Date _____

Today I feel:

_____

My Happiness Scale 1 - 10 _____   I slept _____ hours

I'm looking forward to:

_____

My intention for the day:

_____

SELF-CARE   3 ways I'm going to care for myself:

1) _____

2) _____

3) _____

TODAY'S MINDFUL ACTIVITY

I shower my body with love, gratitude, and kindness.

_____

(or my choice of Mindful Activity)

PEACEFUL PAUSES   🐾 🐾 🐾 🐾 🐾 🐾 🐾 🐾 🐾

_____

(my Peaceful Pause activity)

178

BODY CARE

Hydration

Veggies

"My-Body-Thanks-Me" Foods

_____

Exercise &
Movement:

(time and activity)

Today's appreciation for my body:

_____

TODAY'S REFLECTION

What did I do well today?

_____

_____

_____

What did I learn from a challenging moment?

_____

_____

_____

Three words to celebrate me today: _____

"I am so grateful for my support systems. Here they are. Here's how they support me and add so much to my life."

Enjoy a few moments of meditation

To access, please go to http://bit.ly/EverydayEaseMed

FREE SPACE for journaling and reflection

7

TIME TO REASSESS

While transformation takes place in each moment,
observable evidence takes time.
Be patient and KFG - Keep Freaking Going.

~ Shanti Douglas ~

YEAH!! You made it!! Thank you SO much for all the work you've done over the past six weeks (or longer if that's what you needed). I hope you feel fantastic and are celebrating yourself in **BIG** ways. All the work you've been doing has made a real difference, not just for you, but for everyone else around you.

To keep this amazing path going and stay motivated for more, it's good to take note of how all the little nuggets of time and attention created big shifts. Below are some things you may notice are different since before you began this journey. Check the ones that are true for you and then add your own.

- ✓ Feeling happy and cherished with all the love and self-care you've given yourself
- ✓ It's easier to know what it is that you want and what you don't want
- ✓ Establishing personal boundaries and keeping them without guilt
- ✓ Finding your voice with courage and strength, asking for what you need and want
- ✓ Recognizing that taking care of you is not a selfish act but an act of love and respect
- ✓ Feeling more alive and vibrant in your body
- ✓ Feeling energized by eating healthy food and regularly exercising
- ✓ Since you're drinking more water, your body feels more cohesive with less aches and pains
- ✓ Sleep is deeper and you're feeling more rested
- ✓ Being able to relax when you'd like to and taking quiet moments regularly throughout the day
- ✓ Being in charge of your day instead of your day being in charge of you
- ✓ More easily identifying what's important and what you can let go of
- ✓ Responding to situations without a sense of undo pressure and trusting the practice of patience
- ✓ You no longer use "overwhelmed, overloaded, stressed, burnt-out," to describe yourself
- ✓ Confidently thinking on your feet as you meet the ever-changing situations of the day
- ✓ Greater resilience to change and the muscle of self-efficacy is building
- ✓ Not getting stressed by things that would have bothered you before
- ✓ Laughing out loud for no particular reason

- ✓ Smiling at people and feeling more connected and open-hearted
- ✓ Being more fully present and tuned in to people
- ✓ Getting less distracted and able to focus on the task at hand for longer periods of time
- ✓ Having "real" conversations with people instead of the surface-level jabber
- ✓ Less re-work in your work product
- ✓ Lower blood pressure and more coherent heart rate
- ✓ Shoulders and neck no longer feel like concrete
- ✓ More energy at the end of the day
- ✓ Not feeling so emotionally drained
- ✓ Feeling capable and able
- ✓ Less confusion and chaos
- ✓ Being accepting of your emotions and doing your best to take care of them as they are

- ✓ _____

- ✓ _____

- ✓ _____

- ✓ _____

- ✓ _____

- ✓ _____

Let's take a look now and see how some of the basics have changed. Before you pull out your Fabulous FRESH Five ratings from Chapter 4, jot down your current rating using the same 1 - 10 scale: "1" is extremely poor and "10" is absolutely fantastic. After you've assessed your current state, go back to Chapter 4 to collect your prior ratings and fill them in here.

How have things shifted and changed? What are the highlights of improvement and satisfaction? Where do you feel great and fantastic? Keep celebrating these and reflect on what you stayed committed to that gave great results. For those places where there's modest improvement, don't lose faith or hope. Keep incorporating small changes with the attitude of self-love and care. You've got this!

FABULOUS FRESH FIVE	IN MY LIFE...	PRIOR RATE	CURRENT RATE
Food	I eat clean and healthy food that naturally energizes my body. Meals are nutritionally balanced and in appropriate portion. I enjoy my food with minimal cravings. Sugar and processed foods are not common on my plate.		
Restful SLEEP	I regularly wake feeling rested and refreshed.		
Exercise & MOVEMENT	I exercise my body every day for at least 30 minutes. I feel free, strong, capable, and physically fit, enjoying the movement of my body.		

STRESS MANAGEMENT	I have a positive outlook and I'm able to manage challenging situations in a constructive and appropriate way. I have a supportive community that cares for me.		
HYDRATION	I drink clean water through the day and am rarely thirsty.		

As you move forward, I'd love to hear from you so please stay connected! Share how it's going for you, what insights and inspirations you've found in these pages, where this self-exploration has taken you and given you experiences of joy and contentment, and how I might support your continued awesomeness. You're SO important. I really want to make sure you have all the tools and resources necessary to keep yourself on this amazing path. Feel free to send a note and let me know how things are going Shanti@8limbsHolisticHealth.com. And don't forget to access the meditation recordings at http://bit.ly/EverydayEaseMeditations, enjoying anything else you might find on the website.

Lots of Peace and Love,

Shanti

ACKNOWLEDGEMENTS

I offer a deep bow of gratitude to my Oma, Frieda Osenberg Mayer, a true living Bodhisattva who changed my entire world and made all the difference in my life. Your unconditional love and acceptance have always been the ground from which I've grown. Your Spirit guides me every time I share the precious and powerful practices of peace and love. Thank you.

Lots and lots of love and gratitude also go to my three boys: Mitchell, Everett, and Connor. Thank you for your presence and patience as I was figuring this crazy mess of a life out, making it work as best I could. I'm so happy we're sharing these breaths together and ridiculously proud of the amazing Beings you are. Mitchell, you keep me sharp and intrigued with possibilities through different perspectives. Everett, your fun and free spirit radiates a sense of freedom and unconditional joy. Connor, thanks for that kick in the butt. You're a fellow lion in this life, taking charge and passionately leading with a huge heart. Gratitude also goes to Suki Ball-Dog Douglas, the best dog ever who brings me many amusing moments and lots of smiles.

I also want to offer gratitude to the many friends along the Path who support me unconditionally, have my back, share in my joys, lovingly witness my tears and fears, and continue to cheer me on: my parents Henry and Thea, Amy AevonAestra Gebo, Kirsten Jettinghoff, Bruce Nichols, Joyce Solomon and Pat Maher, Michael Ciborski and Fern Dorresteyn and the ever-growing and loving community of MorningSun Mindfulness Center.

Lastly, thank you to all the people I've met on this journey in life that have helped to shape me to be the person I am - whether that was with love or a lesson of strength. I'm sending you much peace and gratitude.

ABOUT THE AUTHOR

Shanti Douglas is a Mindfulness and HeartMath® Certified Coach, corporate trainer, writer, and the owner of *8 limbs Holistic Health, LLC*. Her mission is to empower others to have greater balance and ease as they navigate their way through stressful times, to help them recognize their strengths with joy, and to create a life fulfilled.

Shanti is passionate about supporting others to gain better physical, mental, and emotional wellness and shares practical, integrative techniques that inspire confidence for lasting change. Over the past decade, she's facilitated over 500 workshops and trainings to Fortune 100 companies on a variety of well-being topics including positivity and stress management, change and resiliency, emotional regulation, emotional and intuitive eating, and self-love and compassion. She is a sought-after speaker and has shared the integration of personal peace practices with over 20,000 people.

Blending her unique and diverse experience and education, Shanti brings a fresh perspective to life's challenges. Her educational background includes degrees in Psychology and Human Services, Masters work in Consciousness Studies, as well as 20+ years of credit and finance management in both private and regulated business industries. Shanti has multiple certifications in health and wellness coaching, yoga, and energy modalities. She's an active member of Buddhist Zen Master Thich Nhat Hanh's Order of Interbeing (www.plumvillage.org) with a life-centered practice of mindfulness. More can be found at www.8limbsholistichealth.com.

In her leisure time, Shanti enjoys connecting with her three fantastic boys, being outdoors and active in nature, playing ball with her amazing dog Suki, and getting together with good friends. Shanti currently resides in picturesque New Hampshire and loves to do on-site workshops and seminars all over the world.